MAKING CHOICES

Exploring Your Approach to SDGs

Miki Tagashira
Fergus Hann
Reiko Fujita

JN125053

NATIONAL
GEOGRAPHIC
LEARNING

Australia · Brazil · Mexico · Singapore · United Kingdom · United States

Making Choices—Exploring Your Approach to SDGs

Miki Tagashira / Fergus Hann / Reiko Fujita

© 2022 Cengage Learning K.K.

ALL RIGHTS RESERVED. No part of this work covered by the copyright herein may be reproduced, transmitted, stored, or used in any form or by any means—graphic, electronic, or mechanical, including but not limited to photocopying, recording, scanning, digitizing, taping, Web distribution, information networks, or information storage and retrieval systems—without the prior written permission of the publisher.

"National Geographic", "National Geographic Society" and the Yellow Border Design are registered trademarks of the National Geographic Society ® Marcas Registradas

The content of this publication has not been approved by the United Nations and does not reflect the views of the United Nations or its officials or Member States.

Photo Credits:
cover: © UN Photo/Cia Pak; 13: © Handout/Getty Images Publicity/Getty Images; 14: © bennymarty/iStock Editorial/Getty Images Plus/Getty Images; 18: © Mathess/iStock Editorial/Getty Images Plus/Getty Images; 24: © ullstein bild/Getty Images; 30: © NurPhoto/Getty Images; 36: © Yongyuan Dai/iStock Unreleased/Getty Images; 42: © Marla Aufmuth/Getty Images Entertainment/Getty Images; 48: © Martchan/iStock Editorial/Getty Images Plus/Getty Images; 54: © Bloomberg/Getty Images; 60: © SOPA Images/Light Rocket/Getty Images; 66: © Thomas Koehler/Photothek/Getty Images; 72: © Agencia Press South/Getty Images News/Getty Images; 78: © saiko3p/iStock Editorial/Getty Images Plus/Getty Images; 84: © Hugh R Hastings/Getty Images News/Getty Images; 90: © Barcroft Media/Getty Images; 96: © Placebo365/iStock Unreleased/Getty Images; 102: © TPG/Getty Images News/Getty Images; 108: © SOPA Images/Light Rocket/Getty Images; 114: © The Sydney Morning Herald/Fairfax Media/Getty Images

For permission to use material from this textbook or product, e-mail to **elt@cengagejapan.com**

ISBN: 978-4-86312-394-6

National Geographic Learning | Cengage Learning K.K.
No. 2 Funato Building 5th Floor
1-11-11 Kudankita, Chiyoda-ku
Tokyo 102-0073
Japan

Tel: 03-3511-4392
Fax: 03-3511-4391

Preface

You may have encountered the term "SDGs" in every aspect of your daily lives since the adoption of the Sustainable Development Goals by the United Nations in 2015. The SDGs are universal goals that every individual, organization, and nation need to incorporate to transform our planet into a better place to live for future generations. Many companies have also started to take initiatives related to the SDGs. For example, straws made of paper are now provided at some fast-food restaurants. When shopping at stores, more people are using their own shopping bags instead of getting plastic bags at the cashier. You have likely been participating in the SDG efforts without even realizing it.

Making Choices is a comprehensive, content-based English language textbook that takes a deeper look into world issues. The activities will help you to build not only vital English language and communication skills, but also a stronger understanding of world problems and some of the proposed solutions.

One of the main aims of this textbook is to help you to acquire English pronunciation and rhythm through shadowing exercises. Step-by-step shadowing exercises train your mouth and ears. Listening to model sentences repeatedly with attention to pronunciation and rhythm will help you to develop your listening skills, and practicing these out loud over and over can help you to develop your speaking skills. The accompanying audio can also help you to practice shadowing in and out of class.

The SDGs are intended to be achieved by 2030. This is not too far in the future for everyone who uses this textbook. By studying the 17 SDGs from different perspectives, we hope that you will develop an interest in the world around you, and become aware of local and global issues. Let's have fun researching, discussing the topics, and doing projects with an ultimate goal of problem solving!

Miki Tagashira
Fergus Hann
Reiko Fujita

Table of Contents

4

Unit Overview

This textbook covers all the 17 SDGs. The main part is divided into 17 units and every unit is based on one of the SDGs. Each unit consists of the six sections described below:

Vocabulary

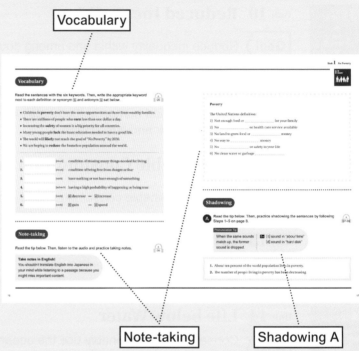

Warm-up

Note-taking

Shadowing A

Warm-up

The unit opener is an opportunity to show what you already know about each of the SDG issues. A series of questions will allow you to start thinking about the goals. You can communicate with your classmates to help to broaden your understanding of the issues.

Vocabulary

Six vocabulary items are keywords selected from the passage in the Shadowing section. These are either academic terms or words related to each specific SDG. Learning the keywords will help you to better understand the content of the passage and the comprehension questions.

Note-taking

The purpose of this task is to develop your note-taking skills while listening to English lectures. In each unit, a tip for note-taking is introduced. You can practice using the tip in the exercise with a part of the passage in the Shadowing section.

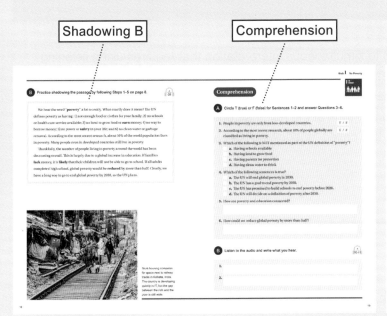

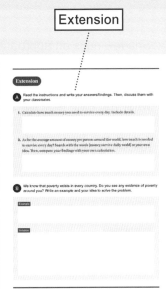

Shadowing

A   A pronunciation tip is introduced to help with listening and speaking. Some example sentences are used to illustrate it. It is then applied in a shadowing practice using two or three sentences from the passage.

B   This section consists of a passage related to one of the SDGs. The passage describes the problems and solutions of the SDG. The purpose of this task is to understand the content of the passage while doing a longer shadowing practice.

Comprehension

A   Various types of questions aim to check your understanding of the passage. You can confirm details and order sequences. You can also make inferences about information in the passage.

B   There are two dictation sentences to check your listening ability and your overall knowledge of the passage.

Extension

A   This section is an opportunity to further research some of the issues related to each of the SDGs. You will also develop your skills in summarizing and reporting the results of your research.

B   This final activity allows you to apply all the information you have learned from the unit through a practical example and possible solutions in your life. If time allows, you will discuss ideas and solutions together with your classmates.

Steps to Shadowing

Shadowing is an approach to simultaneous interpretation that requires using listening and speaking skills at the same time. Empirical research has shown the effectiveness of shadowing practice for learning foreign languages. In the practice, you imitate what you hear exactly. You can look at the text first, but you need to imitate the audio without looking in the end. It is called "shadowing" because it is just like your shadow following you.

How to Practice

Step 1 ▶ Checking

- Read the text and check the vocabulary, grammar, and meanings of each sentence.

Step 2 ▶ Listening

- Look at the text and listen to the entire audio.
- Listen again and put a slash in the text for each pause.

  Ex Listen again **/** and put a slash in the text **/** for each pause.

  *If a sentence is short enough for you to read without a pause, you don't have to add any slashes.

Step 3 ▶ Repeating

- Look at the text and start listening to the audio.
- Stop the audio after each sentence and repeat what you hear.

Step 4 ▶ Overlapping

- Look at the text and start listening to the audio.
- Imitate what you hear simultaneously while listening.

Step 5 ▶ Shadowing

- Without looking at the text, start listening to the audio.
- Imitate what you hear while simultaneously listening.

How to Access the Audio and Video Online

For activities with a headset icon (A/00) or a camera icon (VIDEO),
the audio and video are available at the following website.

https://ngljapan.com/mcs-audiovideo/

You can access the audio and video as outlined below.

❶ Visit the website above.

❷ Click "Audio MP3 (音声ファイル)" or "Video (ビデオ)."

❸ Click the link to the content you would like to listen to or watch.

Use the QR code to directly access the audio and video.

Introduction

SUSTAINABLE DEVELOPMENT GOALS

Warm-up

Look at the icons above and write answers for the following questions. Then, ask the questions to your partner.

1. What do you think these icons mean?

2. Do you think creating these goals is important? Why or why not?

Vocabulary

Read the sentences with the six keywords. Then, write the appropriate keyword next to each definition or synonym ⓢ and antonym ⓐ set below.

A 02

- Governments should promote more healthy and **sustainable** farming methods.
- Cities around the world have gone through rapid **development** in the last 50 years.
- What is the **purpose** of studying these 17 diverse topics?
- It is the duty of national leaders to **protect** people.
- Each country has **distinct** cultural ideas that are interesting to compare.
- The **principal** goal of the organization is to improve the lives of people.

1. _____ [adjective] able to keep something at a constantly safe level

2. _____ [noun] reason for doing something

3. _____ [adjective] first in order of importance

4. _____ [adjective] ⓢ special ↔ ⓐ common

5. _____ [verb] ⓢ defend ↔ ⓐ harm

6. _____ [noun] ⓢ growth ↔ ⓐ destruction

Shadowing

Practice shadowing the passage by following Steps 1–5 on page 8.

A 03

In 2015, the 17 **Sustainable Development** Goals (SDGs) were developed by the United Nations*. The **purpose** of the SDGs is to end suffering, **protect** the environment of the planet, and allow all people to live in peace by 2030.

Although the SDGs are **distinct** and unique, they are connected to each other. If improvements are made in one goal, this will also help to improve the situation in other goals. Goals should be met for all nations and people. A **principal** promise of the SDGs is to "Leave No One Behind." By this, the UN means they will focus more time, energy, and money on the people who need help the most.

*United Nations (UN) is an international organization made up of 193 countries and member states.

Discussion

 A Exchanging opinions is very important to know each other's viewpoints. Listen to the audio and practice talking with your partner.
A
04

> **Jun:** Which of the SDGs do you think are the most important, Mei?
>
> **Mei:** Well, they are all important but I think the most important goal for me is SDG 6 "Clean Water and Sanitation." I feel that SDG 2 "Zero Hunger" is really important as well. What about you, Jun? Which goals are the most important to you?
>
> **Jun:** It's such a difficult thing to choose. I think that SDG 4 "Quality Education" and SDG 2 are the most important goals for me.
>
> **Mei:** Wow, we both chose SDG 2. Why did you choose it, Jun?
>
> **Jun:** Everyone has to eat enough food every day so that we can remain healthy.
>
> **Mei:** I agree. Many children around the world are suffering, so there has to be something that we could do to help them.

B Look at SDGs 1–17 on page 11. Then, choose two goals that are important to you and write the reasons.

- SDG ___ :

- SDG ___ :

C Talk about goals that are important to you and your classmates. Do they have similar opinions with you or not? Complete the chart.

Classmates' Names	Important Goals and Reasons	Comparison to Your Opinions
	• SDG ___ :	Similar / Different
	• SDG ___ :	Similar / Different
	• SDG ___ :	Similar / Different
	• SDG ___ :	Similar / Different
	• SDG ___ :	Similar / Different
	• SDG ___ :	Similar / Different

These rows of flags mark the entrance of the United Nations Offices in Geneva, Switzerland. It has been the main European headquarters of the UN since 1966.

No
Poverty

Warm-up

Write answers for the following questions. Then, ask the questions to your partner.

1. What does the word "poverty" mean to you?

2. What problems do you think people living in poverty have?

3. How many people do you think live in poverty? Fill in the blank below.

I think about   **% of the world population lives in poverty.**

Vocabulary

Read the sentences with the six keywords. Then, write the appropriate keyword next to each definition or synonym ⓢ and antonym ⓐ set below.

- Children in **poverty** don't have the same opportunities as those from wealthy families.
- There are millions of people who **earn** less than one dollar a day.
- Increasing the **safety** of women is a big priority for all countries.
- Many young people **lack** the basic education needed to have a good life.
- The world will **likely** not reach the goal of "No Poverty" by 2030.
- We are hoping to **reduce** the homeless population around the world.

1. [noun] condition of missing many things needed for living

2. [noun] condition of being free from danger or fear

3. [verb] have nothing or not have enough of something

4. [adverb] having a high probability of happening or being true

5. [verb] ⓢ decrease ↔ ⓐ increase

6. [verb] ⓢ gain ↔ ⓐ spend

Note-taking

Read the tip below. Then, listen to the audio and practice taking notes.

Take notes in English!
You shouldn't translate English into Japanese in your mind while listening to a passage because you might miss important content.

Poverty

The United Nations definition:

1) Not enough food or _____ for your family

2) No _____ or health care service available

3) No land to grow food or _____ money

4) No way to _____ money

5) No _____ or safety in your life

6) No clean water or garbage _____

Shadowing

 Read the tip below. Then, practice shadowing the sentences by following Steps 1–5 on page 8.

A
07-08

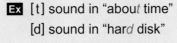

Pronunciation Tip

When the same sounds match up, the former sound is dropped.

Ex [t] sound in "abou*t* time"
[d] sound in "har*d* disk"

1. Abou*t* ten percent of the world population lives in poverty.
2. The number of peop*le* living in poverty has been decreasing.

B Practice shadowing the passage by following Steps 1–5 on page 8.

A
09

We hear the word "**poverty**" a lot recently. What exactly does it mean? The UN defines poverty as having: 1) not enough food or clothes for your family; 2) no schools or health care service available; 3) no land to grow food or **earn** money; 4) no way to borrow money; 5) no power or **safety** in your life; and 6) no clean water or garbage removal. According to the most recent research, about 10% of the world population lives in poverty. Many people even in developed countries still live in poverty.

Thankfully, the number of people living in poverty around the world has been decreasing overall. This is largely due to a global increase in education. If families **lack** money, it is **likely** that their children will not be able to go to school. If all adults completed high school, global poverty would be **reduced** by more than half. Clearly, we have a long way to go to end global poverty by 2030, as the UN plans.

Slum housing competes for space next to railway tracks in Kolkata, India. The country is developing quickly in IT, but the gap between the rich and the poor is still wide.

Comprehension

A Circle T (true) or F (false) for Sentences 1–2 and answer Questions 3–6.

1. People in poverty are only from less-developed countries. T / F

2. According to the most recent research, about 10% of people globally are T / F
classified as living in poverty.

3. Which of the following is NOT mentioned as part of the UN definition of "poverty"?

   a. Having schools available

   b. Having land to grow food

   c. Having parents for protection

   d. Having clean water to drink

4. Which of the following sentences is true?

   a. The UN will end global poverty in 2030.

   b. The UN has a goal to end poverty by 2030.

   c. The UN has promised to build schools to end poverty before 2030.

   d. The UN will decide on a definition of poverty after 2030.

5. How are poverty and education connected?

6. How could we reduce global poverty by more than half?

B Listen to the audio and write what you hear.

A
10-11

1.

2.

Extension

A Read the instructions and write your answers/findings. Then, discuss them with your classmates.

1. Calculate how much money you need to survive every day. Include details.

2. As for the average amount of money per person around the world, how much is needed to survive every day? Search with the words [money survive daily world] or your own idea. Then, compare your findings with your own calculation.

B We know that poverty exists in every country. Do you see any evidence of poverty around you? Write an example and your idea to solve the problem.

Example

Solution

Unit 2

Zero Hunger

Write answers for the following questions. Then, ask the questions to your partner.

1. What does the word "hunger" mean to you?

2. If we don't have enough to eat in our daily life, what do you think could happen to us?

3. How many people do you think are suffering from hunger? Fill in the blank below.

I think about _____ % of the world population is suffering from hunger.

Vocabulary

Read the sentences with the six keywords. Then, write the appropriate keyword next to each definition or synonym ⓢ and antonym ⓐ set below.

- We have to examine different ways to **feed** the growing population.
- There are **negative** feelings about food that is thrown away at buffet restaurants.
- There is limited **access** to food distribution systems in some remote areas.
- There are several solutions to reduce the amount of food that we **waste** every day.
- The video on safe food preparation went **viral**, with more than one million views on YouTube.
- The UN is urging governments to manage their food resources **efficiently**.

1. _____ [adverb]   in a well-organized way

2. _____ [adjective]   spreadable through the internet like a virus

3. _____ [verb]   damage or use something needlessly

4. _____ [verb]   provide food or nutrition for living things

5. _____ [noun]   method or opportunity to reach something

6. _____ [adjective]   ⓢ unfavorable ↔ ⓐ positive

Note-taking

Read the tip below. Then, listen to the audio and practice taking notes.

Keep writing!
You don't have to worry about misspelling when you take notes in English. Writing down the points is more important.

Current Situation on Global Hunger

- The UN:
    - plan to end hunger
    - get food _____ for people through international _____
    - improve _____ for everyone
    - promote healthy ways of farming

- Roughly one-third of all food around the world is _____.

- Campaigns have been created _____ to fight this problem.

Shadowing

 Read the tip below. Then, practice shadowing the sentences by following Steps 1–5 on page 8.

Pronunciation Tip	
When plosive sounds are said together, the former plosive is often not fully pronounced.	Plosive [p] [b] [t] [d] [k] [g]
	Ex [t] sound in "credi*t* card"
	[d] sound in "salt an*d* pepper"

1. They don'*t* get enough food to grow into healthy adults.
2. There are about 300 million fewer hungry people compare*d* to 30 years ago.
3. Their goal is to improve nutrition for everyone an*d* promote healthy ways of farming.

Every day, millions of people are not able to **feed** their families. In 2019, almost 690 million people went to bed hungry. This equals 8.9% of the world population. Hunger affects children's growth in a **negative** way. They don't get enough food to grow into healthy adults. They are often smaller than other children who have not experienced hunger in their lives. They also have more long-lasting health problems. Unfortunately, it is unlikely that the goal of "Zero Hunger" will be reached by 2030. However, the problem of global hunger is improving. There are about 300 million fewer hungry people compared to 30 years ago.

The UN plans to end hunger and get food **access** for people through international cooperation. In addition, their goal is to improve nutrition for everyone and promote healthy ways of farming. Roughly one-third of all food around the world is **wasted**. Campaigns have been created online to fight this problem. For example, one **viral** video featured Egyptian farmers. The video showed them how to farm and market their vegetables more **efficiently**. As a result, the farmers were able to reduce the amount of food waste generated on their farms considerably.

Fruits and vegetables are offered for sale in a farmer's market in Egypt. It is estimated that more than 25% of Egyptians are employed in farming and fishing.

Comprehension

A Circle T (true) or F (false) for Sentences 1–2 and answer Questions 3–6.

1. Most people around the world don't have enough food to eat.   T / F

2. The number of people suffering from hunger around the world is decreasing.   T / F

3. What is the main idea of the passage?
   a. Egyptian farmers are beating hunger by producing videos.
   b. Hunger can affect our growth, but the problem can be reduced.
   c. The UN provides food for people who are suffering from hunger.
   d. We should be aware that a lot of food around the world is wasted.

4. Which of the following sentences would the author agree with?
   a. The goal of "Zero Hunger" will be successfully completed by 2030.
   b. Educational video campaigns have had a positive effect on farming.
   c. The majority of food produced around the world is wasted.
   d. Less than 10% of the world population has enough food to eat.

5. In what two ways does long-term hunger affect children?

6. What was the result of the viral video featuring Egyptian farmers?

B Listen to the audio and write what you hear.   A 18-19

1.

2.

Extension

A Read the instructions and write your answers/findings. Then, discuss them with your classmates.

1. How much food globally is wasted each year? Search with the words [food loss around the world] or your own idea.

2. What exactly did Egyptian farmers do to save food? Search with the words [hunger project Egypt] or your own idea.

B We know that hunger exists in most countries. Do you see any evidence of hunger around you? Write an example and your idea to solve the problem.

Example

Solution

Good Health and Well-being

· ·

Warm-up

Write answers for the following questions. Then, ask the questions to your partner.

1. When was the last time you went to see a doctor? Why did you go?

2. What do you think the most important things for people to lead a healthy life are?

3. What does "well-being" mean to you?

Vocabulary

Read the sentences with the six keywords. Then, write the appropriate keyword next to each definition or synonym ⓢ and antonym ⓐ set below.

- Many diseases can **spread** by physical contact or through the air we breathe.
- The flu is largely **preventable** with the use of vaccines.
- The UN aims to **minimize** the cost of health care around the world.
- Doctors play a **vital** part in keeping people healthy.
- Although medicine for malaria is available, many families still can't **afford** it.
- Exercising regularly has many **beneficial** health effects.

1. [verb] have enough money or able to pay for something

2. [adjective] can be avoided

3. [verb] extend over a large area

4. [adjective] necessary or extremely important

5. [verb] reduce to the smallest possible amount

6. [adjective] ⓢ advantageous ↔ ⓐ harmful

Note-taking

Read the tip below. Then, listen to the audio and practice taking notes.

Organize the information!
Noticing different levels of information such as a topic, sub-topic(s), and details will help you to understand the main ideas of a passage. You can use numbers, colons, bullet points, dashes, and spaces to organize the information.

Health Problems in Developing Countries

1) _____ hospitals, clinics, and medical professionals

2) Trained doctors and nurses _____ to find better-paying jobs

3) Spend very little money on health care

- The health of many people suffers:
  - About 14,000 children under five years old died from _____ illnesses every day in _____.
  - The cost of _____ medical services is more than most people can _____.

Shadowing

A Read the tip below. Then, practice shadowing the sentences by following Steps 1–5 on page 8.

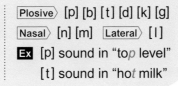

Pronunciation Tip

When a plosive sound is followed by a nasal/lateral sound, the plosive is often not fully pronounced.

Plosive⟩ [p] [b] [t] [d] [k] [g]
Nasal⟩ [n] [m] Lateral⟩ [l]
Ex [p] sound in "top level"
[t] sound in "hot milk"

1. Trained doctors and nurses find better-paying jobs in developed countries.
2. This means that medical services, medicine, and vaccines should be available to everyone.

B Practice shadowing the passage by following Steps 1–5 on page 8.

The **spread** of malaria and many other illnesses is **preventable**. There are things that could be done to **minimize** health problems and deaths. In developing countries, there are few hospitals, clinics, and medical professionals. Trained doctors and nurses from these countries leave to find better-paying jobs in developed countries. Governments of some developing countries spend very little money on health care. The health of many people suffers because of these reasons. This is particularly true of new mothers and children. About 14,000 children under five years old died from preventable illnesses every day in 2019. Sadly, in some countries, the cost of **vital** medical services is more than most people can **afford**. Deaths would be reduced if people had easier access to medicine.

The UN believes that one of the most important ways to keep people healthy is through a universal health care system. This means that medical services, medicine, and vaccines should be available to everyone even if they can't afford it. As of 2021, 116 countries have a universal health care system. Providing free health care reduces illnesses and deaths. Things are slowly improving. Since 1990, the number of childhood deaths has decreased by more than half. This is because of improvements in health and medical services. Healthy people are **beneficial** to the economy of a country.

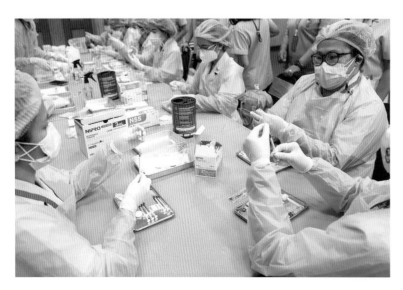

Health workers prepare doses of the Pfizer vaccine for the COVID-19 coronavirus for high school students in Bangkok, Thailand.

Comprehension

A   Circle T (true) or F (false) for Sentences 1–2 and answer Questions 3–6.

1. There is nothing we can do to stop young children from dying.   T / F

2. Some developing countries suffer from a lack of doctors and nurses.   T / F

3. Which of the following sentences is NOT true?
   a. If medicine were more easily available, fewer people would die from malaria.
   b. A universal health care system would help people in developing countries.
   c. There have been improvements in medical services in developing countries.
   d. The number of childhood deaths is increasing in developing countries.

4. Which health care problem is NOT mentioned in the passage?
   a. Many trained medical professionals leave developing countries.
   b. There is a lack of hospitals and clinics in many countries around the world.
   c. Vaccines are researched and produced in developed countries.
   d. Some governments do not spend much money on health care.

5. Why do doctors and nurses from developing countries move abroad?

6. What is an advantage of a country having a universal health care system?

B   Listen to the audio and write what you hear.

A
25-26

1.

2.

A Read the instructions and write your answers/findings. Then, discuss them with your classmates.

1. Research some infectious diseases and choose one of them. What is the disease name and its cause(s)?

2. Research some information about Doctors Without Borders. Who are they? What do they do?

B Pandemics can greatly affect our well-being. What personal/social/medical/economic/global problems have you seen arising due to COVID-19? Write an example and your idea to solve the problem.

Example

Solution

Quality Education

Warm-up

Write answers for the following questions. Then, ask the questions to your partner.

1. Do you feel you have had a good education so far? Why do you think so?

2. Imagine you have never had access to education. What would your life be like?

3. How many people do you think can't read or write? Fill in the blank below.

I think about ____ % of the world population can't read or write.

Vocabulary

Read the sentences with the six keywords. Then, write the appropriate keyword next to each definition or synonym ⓢ and antonym ⓐ set below.

A
27

- Poverty is strongly connected to the education **rate**.
- This **statistic** shows that many people pay more than 25% of their wages for children's education.
- Everyone in my family is **literate** because we had a good education.
- Family income is a **factor** for why some girls don't go to school.
- Gender **inequality** negatively affects education and access to work for women.
- Opportunities for education have improved over the last **decade**.

1. [noun] period of ten years

2. [adjective] able to read and write

3. [noun] percentage of something in a group

4. [noun] reason or element as the cause of something

5. [noun] figure or result from research

6. [noun] ⓢ unfairness ↔ ⓐ fairness

Note-taking

Read the tip below. Then, listen to the audio and practice taking notes.

A
28

Pay attention to the percentage!
Percentage or rate is used in many statistics to compare things. Therefore, noticing the difference in a number helps you to find important facts in a passage.

Literacy Rate

Area: • World _____%
       • Developed Countries   99%
       • South Asia   73%
       • Sub-Saharan Africa   _____%

Gender (Females/Males): • World   F: 83%   M: _____%
                          • Yemen   F: _____%   M: 85%
                          • India   F: _____%   M: _____%

• •

Shadowing

 Read the tip below. Then, practice shadowing the sentences by following Steps 1–5 on page 8.

> **Pronunciation Tip**
>
> When a plosive sound is followed by a fricative sound, the plosive is often not fully pronounced.
>
> Plosive〉 [p] [b] [t] [d] [k] [g]
> Fricative〉 [f] [v] [ə] [ð] [s] [z] [ʃ] [ʒ] [h]
> **Ex** [p] sound in "to*p* floor"
> [t] sound in "si*t* there"

1. Everyone shoul*d* have access to education.

2. Parents can't afford to sen*d* their children to school.

B Practice shadowing the passage by following Steps 1–5 on page 8.

A
31

Everyone should have access to education. It is a basic human right*. The level of education is often measured by the literacy **rate***. According to the most recent **statistics**, the global literacy rate is only 86% of the world population. 99% of people in developed countries are **literate**, compared to 73% in South Asia, and only 65% in Sub-Saharan Africa. Poverty is one of the main **factors**. Parents can't afford to send their children to school. Another **inequality** in education is gender. The global literacy rate for females is only 83% compared to 90% for males. The gap is much larger in many countries. For example, the most recent data for Yemen shows that only 55% of females are literate compared to 85% of males. In India, the literacy rate is 66% for females and 82% for males.

However, some progress has been made. Since 1960, the global literacy rate has been increasing steadily by more than 7% per **decade**. Access to education in developing countries has been improved with the construction of schools. In addition, better opportunities for training have resulted in an increased number of teachers. The UN wants everyone to have free primary and secondary education by 2030. Research shows that educated adults take better care of their families. As a result, education is the key to lifting families and nations out of poverty.

*A human right is a standard that recognizes and protects the dignity of all human beings.
*Literacy rate is the percentage of the adult population aged 15 and older that can read and write.

Children in Siem Reap have English lessons from volunteers at a school called New Bridge for Cambodia. The NGO offers free education for disadvantaged students.

Comprehension

A Circle T (true) or F (false) for Sentences 1–2 and answer Questions 3–6.

1. Globally, more than 20% of people over the age of 15 can't read and write.   T / F

2. The percentage of literate adults has increased since 1960.   T / F

3. What is the main idea of the passage?
    a. Geographical and gender inequalities in education are improving overall.
    b. Most developing countries have lower literacy rates than developed countries.
    c. Poverty has a negative effect on children being able to go to school.
    d. Training teachers and building schools have improved the literacy rate in developed countries.

4. Which is NOT true about providing free primary and secondary education?
    a. More parents can send their children to school.
    b. Educated people can provide a better life for their children.
    c. Countries with educated populations have stronger economies.
    d. It has little effect on the literacy rate.

5. What are two reasons that the literacy rate in developing countries has been increasing?

6. What educational goal does the UN want to achieve by 2030?

B Listen to the audio and write what you hear.

A
32-33

1.

2.

Extension

A Read the instructions and write your answers/findings. Then, discuss them with your classmates.

1. What are the causes of inequal or low-quality education around the world?

2. Search with the words [project UNESCO] and choose one educational project. What is the project name? What is it about?

B Inequality in education exists in many countries. Do you see any evidence of that in your schools or community? Write an example and your idea to solve the problem.

Example

Solution

Gender Equality

• •

Warm-up

Write answers for the following questions. Then, ask the questions to your partner.

1. Do you feel you have had equal gender opportunities at school? Explain.

2. What are some examples of gender inequality? Where can they happen?

3. What would be an ideal relationship between a husband and a wife for you?

Vocabulary

Read the sentences with the six keywords. Then, write the appropriate keyword next to each definition or synonym ⓢ and antonym ⓐ set below.

- Minorities like the LGBTQ community experience **discrimination** in finding jobs.
- **Domestic** arguments could mean serious trouble for husbands and wives.
- My mother never asks my brother to do **chores** like cooking and doing the laundry.
- Women suffer a higher **proportion** of violence from unemployed spouses.
- Females report that they make a lower **wage** for doing the same work as males.
- **Significantly** more couples are now keeping their original surnames after marriage.

1. _____ [adjective] relating to the house or family

2. _____ [noun] routine tasks, especially around the house

3. _____ [noun] unfair treatment or bias against a certain group of people

4. _____ [noun] payment earned for work completed

5. _____ [noun] ratio of one part to another part

6. _____ [adverb] ⓢ considerably ↔ ⓐ slightly

Note-taking

Read the tip below. Then, listen to the audio and practice taking notes.

Pay attention to timelines!
Dates and years are necessary for comparing statistics. Therefore, noticing timelines helps you to find important facts in a passage.

Proportion of Women

- Management jobs around the world: 2000   25%

                                         _____   28%

- Gender wage gap: _____   earned ____% of salary that men made

                      _____   ____%

- The gap has decreased _____ over time.

. . . .

Shadowing

 Read the tip below. Then, practice shadowing the sentences by following
Steps 1–5 on page 8.

Pronunciation Tip	
When a plosive/fricative sound is followed by a vowel sound, both sounds are often linked together.	**Plosive** [p] [b] [t] [d] [k] [g] **Fricative** [f] [v] [e] [ð] [s] [z] [ʃ] [ʒ] [h] **Ex** [v] and a vowel sounds in "li*ve i*n" [z] and a vowel sounds in "three hour*s a* week"

1. Domestic work can resul*t i*n women having less work experience outside the home.

2. Women earne*d a*bout 60 percen*t o*f the salary that men ma*de i*n the same job.

B Practice shadowing the passage by following Steps 1–5 on page 8.

A
38

Violence and **discrimination** against women are widespread around the world. For example, 49 countries still lack laws to protect women from **domestic** violence as of 2021. In their lifetime, almost 33% of women have suffered from physical or sexual violence by a husband or partner. Moreover, domestic work can result in women having less work experience outside the home. In the US, adult women spend almost 40 hours a week cooking, cleaning, and taking care of family members. On the other hand, adult men spend less than 25 hours a week doing the same **chores**.

The success of the SDGs depends heavily on the goal of "Gender Equality" being reached. Improving the lives of women affects everyone's income, education, and health. According to a survey of 141 countries, the percentage of countries that have laws protecting women from domestic violence increased from 71% to 76% between 2013 and 2017. The **proportion** of women in management jobs around the world in 2000 was about 25%, whereas the statistic grew to about 28% in 2019. There have also been improvements in the gender **wage** gap. In 1980, women earned about 60% of the salary that men made in the same job. In 2019, the figure had increased to 82%. The gap has decreased **significantly** over time, but there is still a long way to go to close the gap.

Nobel Peace Prize winner Malala Yousafzai speaks at a conference for women in Boston, US. She is an activist for female education and a UN Messenger of Peace.

Comprehension

A Circle T (true) or F (false) for Sentences 1–2, complete Sentences 3–4, and answer Questions 5–6.

1. Domestic violence has only been reported in 49 countries.　　　T / F

2. Almost 33% of women have experienced domestic violence in their lifetime.　　T / F

3. The number of women in management positions ...
   - **a.** varies by the governments of each country.
   - **b.** depends on the public image that each company wants to have.
   - **c.** is an example of discrimination against women.
   - **d.** is a reflection of the number of women with paid employment.

4. In the future, the gender wage gap will most likely ...
   - **a.** increase based on the strength of the economy.
   - **b.** increase as more women will be working inside the home.
   - **c.** decrease as laws require companies to raise wages for women.
   - **d.** decrease as women spend more time taking care of children.

5. What is a disadvantage of women spending more time on domestic chores than men?

6. Why is the goal of "Gender Equality" so important to the success of the SDGs?

B Listen to the audio and write what you hear.

A
39-40

1.

2.

Extension

A Read the instructions and write your answers/findings. Then, discuss them with your classmates.

1. Research the "Global Gender Gap Report" and find the rank of your country in terms of gender equality.

2. Child marriage is still a common practice in many regions. Research some information about it.

B Do you think your country has achieved a high level of gender equality? Which aspects still require improvements? Write an example and your idea to solve the problem.

Example

Solution

44

6 CLEAN WATER AND SANITATION

Clean Water and Sanitation

Warm-up

Write answers for the following questions. Then, ask the questions to your partner.

1. For what purposes do you use water in your daily life?

2. How much water do you think you use daily? How many 2-liter plastic bottles would that be?

3. Without a clean water supply or bottled water, what would your life be like? What could you do to get clean water?

Vocabulary

Read the sentences with the six keywords. Then, write the appropriate keyword next to each definition or synonym ⓢ and antonym ⓐ set below.

- The world water **crisis** affects the health of millions of people.
- People **require** clean water for almost every aspect of their lives.
- Handwashing with soap and clean water would reduce the number of those suffering from **diseases**.
- Epidemics can easily spread by having poor methods of **sanitation**.
- We need a strategy to **achieve** access to clean water for everyone.
- Flooding from storms can **substantially** reduce the quality of drinking water.

1. _____ [verb]   need something necessary

2. _____ [noun]   wastewater treatment or public health

3. _____ [verb]   reach a goal successfully

4. _____ [noun]   situation of strong difficulty or danger

5. _____ [noun]   illnesses or serious health problems

6. _____ [adverb] ⓢ considerably ↔ ⓐ somewhat

Note-taking

Read the tip below. Then, listen to the audio and practice taking notes.

Notice the transition words!
Transition words are often used when comparing things or adding more information. Therefore, noticing those words helps you to understand the context of a passage.

Clean Water and Safe Sanitation

1) Since 2000: Access to _____ has

   increased by 1.8 billion

2) _____, 2.1 billion people gained access to

   _____ for toilets and wastewater.

   - It _____ increased: Eastern and South-Eastern

     Asia from ____% to ____%

   - _____, there are still many areas _____

     access to safe sanitation.

   - Access in Sub-Saharan _____ has not increased

     significantly.

Example Transition Words
Comparison/Contrast
although
compared to
however
in comparison
in contrast
likewise
nevertheless
on the other hand
similarly
whereas
Addition
additionally
also
furthermore
in addition
moreover

Shadowing

 Read the tip below. Then, practice shadowing the sentences by following
Steps 1–5 on page 8.

A
43-44

Pronunciation Tip

When a nasal sound is followed by a vowel sound, both sounds are often linked together.

Nasal〉 [n] [m]
Ex [n] and a vowel sounds in "sig*n u*p"
[m] and a vowel sounds in "infor*m u*s"

1. I*n a*ddition to the water supply problem, 3.6 billion people lack safe sanitation.

2. Recently, there have been so*me i*mprovements, though.

B Practice shadowing the passage by following Steps 1–5 on page 8.

The global water **crisis** has deepened over the last century. We use a lot more water per person than we used to. The amount of water we use globally has increased twice as fast as the population has grown. We **require** clean water for drinking, cooking, and health services. Access to clean water also reduces **diseases**. Still, 2 billion people live without it every day. In addition to the water supply problem, 3.6 billion people, about half of the world population, lack safe **sanitation** for toilets and wastewater. In some developing countries, many families and communities share one toilet. This can also cause diseases to spread easily.

The world is far behind in **achieving** the goal for clean water and safe sanitation for everyone. Recently, there have been some improvements, though. Since the year 2000, the number of people globally with access to clean water has increased by 1.8 billion. Similarly, 2.1 billion people gained access to safe sanitation for toilets and wastewater. It also increased **substantially** in Eastern and South-Eastern Asia from 21% to 60% of the population. However, there are still many areas without access to safe sanitation. Access in Sub-Saharan Africa has not increased significantly and it is still a major problem.

Women and young girls collect water from a rain water pool in Gayo, Ethiopia. The water is cleaned with tablets before use.

Comprehension

A Circle T (true) or F (false) for Sentences 1–2, complete Sentences 3–4, and answer Questions 5–6.

1. We use the same amount of water per person as we did 100 years ago.　　T / F

2. About 50% of the world population lives without safe sanitation.　　T / F

3. Since the year 2000, ...
   - **a.** the goal for achieving clean water worldwide has been reached.
   - **b.** there has been little improvement to safe sanitation.
   - **c.** the number of people with access to clean water has increased.
   - **d.** more people have acquired clean water than safe sanitation.

4. The number of people suffering from diseases would decrease ...
   - **a.** if people used less water in their daily lives.
   - **b.** if the world population increased.
   - **c.** if clean water and sanitation were available to everyone.
   - **d.** if communities shared sanitation facilities like toilets.

5. What three daily tasks mentioned require clean water?

6. How has access to safe sanitation in Eastern and South-Eastern Asia changed over the last 20 years?

B Listen to the audio and write what you hear.

A
46-47

1.

2.

Extension

A Read the instructions and write your answers/findings. Then, discuss them with your classmates.

1. What are the reasons why so many people can't get clean water easily?

2. What efforts are being made to bring clean water to needy areas? Search with the words [bring clean water].

B Climate change is causing water shortages around the world, and it is important to save water. What things could you do to save water? Write an example and a collaborative effort you could do.

Example

Collaborative Effort

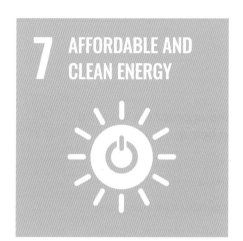

Affordable and Clean Energy

Warm-up

Write answers for the following questions. Then, check your answers with your partner.

1. "Clean energy" is also called "renewable energy." Try to identify if the following sources are renewable or non-renewable.

solar gas thermal wind coal wave oil water nuclear

Renewable	Non-renewable

2. What do you think of clean energy? List its advantages and disadvantages.

Advantages	Disadvantages

Vocabulary

Read the sentences with the six keywords. Then, write the appropriate keyword next to each definition or synonym ⓢ and antonym ⓐ set below.

A 48

- Solar energy will **generate** a substantial amount of electricity around the world.
- Burning fossil fuels is a major environmental **issue** that needs to be addressed.
- Automakers should **invest** more money in the development of electric vehicles.
- Wind is quickly becoming a very popular alternative **source** of energy.
- Researching and developing renewable energy is a **financial** challenge.
- Studies **predict** that the new electric power plant will be good for the economy.

1. _____ [adjective] relating to money or the economy

2. _____ [verb] state something that will happen in the future

3. _____ [verb] use valuable things for profit or advantage

4. _____ [noun] origin of something

5. _____ [noun] ⓢ problem ↔ ⓐ solution

6. _____ [verb] ⓢ produce ↔ ⓐ destroy

Note-taking

Read the tip below. Then, listen to the audio and practice taking notes.

A 49

Pay attention to big numbers!
The sounds of "million" and "billion" are similar but the meanings are completely different. In order to avoid confusion, make sure to catch those words and write down the numbers.

Access to Clean Energy

- 2010: About _____ people   no access to electricity

- 9 years later: Reduced to _____
  - Still _____ in providing sources

- Since 2010: ____% increase   financial aid for developing countries

Shadowing

 Read the tip below. Then, practice shadowing the sentences by following Steps 1–5 on page 8.

Pronunciation Tip

A word starting with a vowel sound and ending with a consonant sound can be linked with a preceding word and a following word. The three words sound like one unit.

Ex "che*ck it o*ut"
"ma*de in A*merica"

1. There has been an improvemen*t in a*ccess to clean energy.

2. Th*e amount of* solar energy produced in India has doubled since 2017.

It is a fact that many people around the world still rely on electricity **generated** from fossil fuels*. Using them for cooking inside the home is the most affordable option in developing countries. However, it causes air pollution, and often results in serious health problems. Although about 66% of the world population cooks with clean energy, it is not enough to reduce the problems of using fossil fuels. Budget is also a major **issue** in researching alternative natural resources. Developing countries have a limited amount of money to **invest** in new types of energy.

Actually, there has been an improvement in access to clean energy. In 2010, about 1.2 billion people had no access to electricity globally. Nine years later, the number has been reduced to 759 million. However, the world is still behind in providing **sources** of clean energy that everyone can afford. Since 2010, there has been a 32% increase in **financial** aid for developing countries to use clean energy. Projects using clean energy are now growing fastest in developing countries. For example, the amount of solar energy produced in India has doubled since 2017. Accordingly, India's use of coal has declined each year since 2018. It is **predicted** to continue decreasing.

*Fossil fuels include oil/petroleum, coal, kerosene, and natural gas that are burned to produce energy.

A coal-fired power station in Mpumalanga, South Africa. Economic development tends to be favored over environmental issues, particularly in developing countries.

Comprehension

A Circle T (true) or F (false) for Sentences 1–2, complete Sentences 3–4, and answer Questions 5–6.

1. Reducing fossil fuel use will improve people's health.   T / F

2. The majority of people around the world cook with clean energy sources.   T / F

3. Using fossil fuels for cooking is ...
    a. only permitted outside of people's homes.
    b. too expensive for people in developing countries.
    c. a good example of a renewable energy source.
    d. the cheapest alternative in developing countries.

4. India is ...
    a. donating money to developing countries for energy projects.
    b. reducing the number of people who rely on electricity.
    c. replacing the use of fossil fuels with solar energy.
    d. depending on international aid to solve its energy problems.

5. Why is it difficult for people in developing countries to reduce fossil fuel use?

6. What are the effects of clean energy projects in developing countries? Write an example.

B Listen to the audio and write what you hear.

A
53-54

1.

2.

Extension

A Read the instructions and write your answers/findings. Then, discuss them with your classmates.

1. Research some information about wind farms in your country. Where are they? How many wind turbines are there? How much energy is generated?

2. Many renewable energy projects have been carried out in developing countries. What are they trying to do? Search with the words [renewable energy project].

B Do you know any clean energy being used around you? Write an example and your idea to increase its use.

Example

Improvement

Decent Work and Economic Growth

Write answers for the following questions. Then, ask the questions to your partner.

1. Suppose you work part-time. Describe your work environment such as hourly wage, work hours, benefits, and/or how busy it is.

2. When you have a full-time job in the future, will you mind working overtime? Why?

3. What does "decent work" mean? What factors make work decent or indecent?

Vocabulary

Read the sentences with the six keywords. Then, write the appropriate keyword next to each definition or synonym ⓢ and antonym ⓐ set below.

- The judge determined that the **employer** had abused workers.
- My **situation** is difficult, as I'm not attending school and can't find full-time work.
- People in some prisons endure forced **labor** for years without payment.
- Many organizations help people to find **decent** jobs that are free from problems.
- The **aim** of the NGO is to end low wages for migrants around the world.
- What **measures** can be taken to protect informal workers?

1. _____ [noun]   person or company that hires people to work

2. _____ [noun]   actions or steps taken to solve a problem

3. _____ [noun]   condition that exists at a certain time

4. _____ [noun]   goal for doing something

5. _____ [noun]   physical or mental performance to make money

6. _____ [adjective] ⓢ proper ↔ ⓐ terrible

Note-taking

Read the tip below. Then, listen to the audio and practice taking notes. Write the appropriate symbol in the [   ].

Use symbols!
There are many symbols you can use for writing down key points.
This can save time when you are taking notes.

Global Economy

Slowdown: Started a decade before COVID-19

1) Companies: Struggling to survive

- [   ] Treating workers poorly

2) Employees:

- Forced to work too many hours in _____ conditions

- [   ] get _____ enough for work

- About _____ people [   ] informal jobs:
  Construction workers, cleaners, housekeepers, nannies

- × _____ by governments

Useful Symbols	
→	because
	cause
	go to
	lead to
	move to
	next
	then
←	caused by
	result of
+, &	also
	and
×	no
	not
w/	with
w/o	without

Shadowing

 A Read the tip below. Then, practice shadowing the sentences by following Steps 1–5 on page 8.

A
57-58

Pronunciation Tip

Be-verbs such as "is," "are," "was," and "were" are often pronounced quickly and weakly.

1. They *are* often not protected by governments.
2. Providing decent, full-time work for everyone *is* also important.

B Practice shadowing the passage by following Steps 1–5 on page 8.

A
59

The slowdown in the global economy had already started a decade before the COVID-19 pandemic. Many companies have been struggling to survive. This can often lead to **employers** treating their workers poorly. Employees may be forced to work too many hours in terrible conditions. They may also not get paid enough for their work. This applies to about 2 billion people with informal jobs such as construction workers, cleaners, housekeepers, or nannies. They are often not protected by governments. This **situation** also creates another problem. Child **labor** affects 152 million children worldwide; 88 million boys and 64 million girls. Most of them start working as their parents don't earn enough money to support them.

The growth of the global economy depends on increasing access to education. In addition, providing **decent**, full-time work for everyone is also important. The International Labor Organization (ILO) works together with the UN and governments to improve the lives of workers. They **aim** to promote decent working conditions. They also fight for employment protection and minimum wages for workers. By increasing access to education and other **measures**, child labor has decreased by 38% in the last 10 years. However, there is still a long way to go.

An eight-year-old boy works at a brick breaking yard in Dhaka, Bangladesh. Child laborers in Bangladesh typically earn less than US$2.00 per day.

Comprehension

A Circle T (true) or F (false) for Sentences 1–2 and answer Questions 3–6.

1. Working conditions depend partly on the economy. T / F

2. Poverty is one of the main causes of child labor. T / F

3. Which of the following sentences is true?
   - **a.** All workers can work as many hours as they want to.
   - **b.** All workers are protected by governments.
   - **c.** Some workers don't get the wages they deserve.
   - **d.** No workers have completed their education.

4. Which of the following sentences is NOT mentioned about the ILO?
   - **a.** It wants to improve the lives of workers around the world.
   - **b.** It is interested in establishing secure jobs for workers.
   - **c.** It believes that there should be a basic payment for workers.
   - **d.** It has helped to increase the number of children with jobs.

5. What are two changes that would improve the global economy?

6. What would happen if more parents earned enough money to support their children?

B Listen to the audio and write what you hear.

A
60-61

1.

2.

Extension

A Read the instructions and write your answers/findings. Then, discuss them with your classmates.

1. The accident at Rana Plaza in Bangladesh is a famous example of people being victimized in a dangerous work environment. Research some information about it.

2. Economic growth is not well-balanced around the world. Search with the words [Doughnut Economics] and find the image of the doughnut. What are your thoughts about this?

B We know that "decent work" is strongly related to "access to education" and "gender equality." How are they related? Write your ideas.

Relation to "access to education"

Relation to "gender equality"

9

Industry, Innovation and Infrastructure

Warm-up

Write answers for the following questions. Then, ask the questions to your partner.

1. What kind of industry do you want to work for in the future? Why?

2. There are many companies incorporating SDGs. Do you know any examples? What are they doing?

3. Improvement of infrastructure is an important aspect of SDG 9. Do you know the meaning of "infrastructure"? Give some examples.

Vocabulary

Read the sentences with the six keywords. Then, write the appropriate keyword next to each definition or synonym ⑤ and antonym ⓐ set below.

- The success of the company depends on a strong transportation **industry**.
- Malaria has had a very negative **effect** on the economy.
- The farmers' total **income** will increase if they install an improved water system.
- **Rural** populations tend to move to cities to find work.
- The small fashion company had an **ambitious** plan to expand to other countries.
- The economic situation on the African **continent** has been improving overall.

1. _____ [noun]   any of the world's big areas of land

2. _____ [noun]   change as a result of an action or event

3. _____ [noun]   money received for work completed

4. _____ [noun]   activity to produce necessary things for people's lives

5. _____ [adjective] relating to the countryside

6. _____ [adjective] ⑤ major ↔ ⓐ minor

Note-taking

Read the tip below. Then, listen to the audio and practice taking notes.

Make the words shorter!
When you listen to a passage, you don't need to write down every word you hear. Using abbreviations is the best way to save time. For example, use only consonants "lsn" for "listen" and capital letters "HW" for "homework."

Manufacturing Industry

Growth: Slow over last decade

- Prob for employment
- 2019: 14% _____ around _____
- COVID-19: Neg efct
  - Decreased to _____% by mid-2020
  - Many job + income losses in smaller biz
- To help smaller biz:
  - Non-profit microloan: Kiva, _____
  - Allow anyone to lend money _____

Useful Abbreviations
biz = business
efct = effect
neg = negative
OL = online
prob = problem
US = the United States
wkr = worker
wld = world

Shadowing

 A Read the tip below. Then, practice shadowing the sentences by following Steps 1–5 on page 8.

A
64-65

Pronunciation Tip

Auxiliary verbs such as "should" and "may" are often pronounced quickly and weakly. Also, the negative part "n't" is shortened in speech.

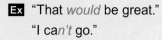

Ex "That *would* be great."
"I ca*n't* go."

1. People *have* lent hundreds of millions of dollars through Kiva.
2. Smaller businesses are*n't* able to develop properly.

Growth in the manufacturing **industry** has been slow over the last decade. This is a problem, as it is very important for employment. In 2019, 14% of workers around the world had manufacturing jobs. However, the COVID-19 pandemic had a negative **effect** and the percentage decreased to 11.5% by mid-2020. There were many job and **income** losses, particularly in smaller businesses. As a result, they had to borrow money from banks to survive, which is usually expensive. To help smaller businesses to borrow money cheaply, there are non-profit microloan companies, like Kiva from the United States. They allow anyone to lend money online to smaller businesses in the manufacturing industry in dozens of countries. People have lent hundreds of millions of dollars through Kiva. Smaller companies use the borrowed money to hire employees and sell products.

A second problem in the manufacturing industry is the lack of infrastructure. For example, the manufacturing industry depends on transportation. Many people living in **rural** areas in developing countries lack decent roads, so smaller businesses aren't able to develop properly. Infrastructure development projects are also helping to solve the problem. One **ambitious** example is the Trans-African Highway network. Nine connected highways are currently being constructed across the **continent**. The goal is to support the manufacturing industry, thereby reducing poverty in Africa.

A shoemaker runs a shop in the old town in Marrakech, Morocco. He opened up the small business with the help of a microloan.

Comprehension

A Circle T (true) or F (false) for Sentences 1–2, complete Sentence 3, and answer Questions 4–6.

1. In 2020, 14% of all workers were employed in the manufacturing industry. T / F

2. Some smaller businesses use bank loans to stay open. T / F

3. The Trans-African Highway network is …
   a. connected to other continents.
   b. a road across Africa.
   c. not yet fully completed.
   d. being paid for by microloans.

4. Which of the following sentences is NOT true about the manufacturing industry?
   a. There was financial damage caused to the industry by the pandemic.
   b. Smaller businesses were more affected by the pandemic than larger businesses.
   c. The manufacturing industry is very important for employment.
   d. There is a lack of workers willing to work in the industry.

5. Why is borrowing money from a microloan company better than borrowing from a bank?

6. What is the effect of a lack of roads in rural areas for smaller businesses?

B Listen to the audio and write what you hear.

A
67-68

1.

2.

Extension

A Read the instructions and write your answers/findings. Then, discuss them with your classmates.

1. Innovations are keys for improving our society and environment. Think of three innovations in the past you think are important. Why do you think so?

2. There are a lot of innovations contributing to SDGs. Research some examples.

B You have learned that there are many different problems around the world such as poverty, energy, water, or education. Write an example around you and your idea to solve the problem through innovation.

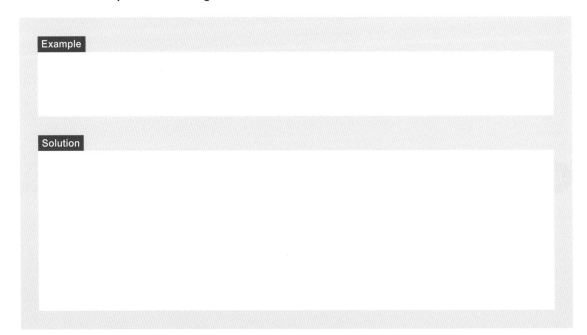

Example

Solution

68

Unit 10

Reduced Inequalities

....

Warm-up

Match the types of inequality with the explanations. Then, check the answers with your partner.

1. educational inequality

2. gender inequality

3. health care inequality

4. income inequality

5. regional inequality

a. People don't have equal rights or opportunities, depending on whether they are male or female.
b. Wages are distributed unevenly in every country. A few people are extremely rich, but there are many poor people.
c. Due to lack of proper registration or money, people have no access to medicine.
d. People in the cities enjoy better services and opportunities than those in rural areas.
e. People have no chance to study because of poverty and other reasons.

Vocabulary

Read the sentences with the six keywords. Then, write the appropriate keyword next to each definition or synonym ⓢ and antonym ⓐ set below.

B / 02

- Policies on gender and income inequality were updated in 2005 and 2020, **respectively**.
- The government will **reverse** its previous decision on immigration.
- The NGO fights any **violation** of human rights.
- He came to this country as a **refugee**, and was able to live a better life.
- The film will **document** how gender inequality affects women.
- The lack of educated women in the country has become a **high-profile** issue.

1.   [noun]   person who leaves his/her country to avoid discrimination

2.   [adjective]   attracting a lot of attention in public

3.   [noun]   act of doing something that is not allowed by law

4.   [verb]   record information

5.   [adverb]   in the order mentioned

6.   [verb]   ⓢ overturn ↔ ⓐ uphold

Note-taking

Read the tip below. Then, listen to the audio and practice taking notes.

B / 03

Use more abbreviations!
There are other ways to make abbreviations. For example, you can write "info" for "information" using the first part of the word. The word "government" can be "govt" using the beginning and last letters.

Educational Inequality

- b/w _____ : 49.5%   PK ppl   completed _____
                  95.8%   S-KOR ppl

- _____ : PK   M 52.4%, F _____ %

- COVID-19 _____ 10 yrs _____

Useful Abbreviations

b/w = between
cntry = country
F = female
gndr = gender
HS = high school
M = male
PK = Pakistan
     Pakistani
ppl = people
prog = progress
rvs = reverse
S-KOR = South Korea
        South Korean
w/n = within
yr = year

 Shadowing

A Read the tip below. Then, practice shadowing the sentences by following Steps 1–5 on page 8.

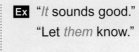

Pronunciation Tip

Pronouns such as "it" and "his" are often pronounced quickly and weakly.

Ex "*It* sounds good."
"Let *them* know."

1. *It* is double the number of refugees documented in 2010.
2. *Their* stories inform *us* of the troubles that refugees face.

Many types of inequality exist in our society. One of them is educational inequality between countries. For example, only 49.5% of Pakistani people have completed high school, compared to 95.8% of South Korean people. There is also gender inequality within each country. For instance, the percentages of males and females in Pakistan who have completed high school are 52.4% and 46.2%, **respectively**. Although in general, inequality had been decreasing globally, the COVID-19 pandemic is said to have **reversed** 10 years of progress.

A major cause of inequality is discrimination among people based on religion, race, gender, and social position. Inequality can lead to conflict and human rights **violations**, particularly in less developed countries. This results in an increase in **refugees** from those countries. Refugee issues are a central part of SDG 10. In mid-2020, there were 24 million refugees, the most ever recorded. It is double the number of refugees **documented** in 2010. People have become more aware of refugee issues through such efforts as the formation of the IOC Refugee Olympic Team. The **high-profile** team competed for the first time at the Rio de Janeiro Olympics. The media has reported widely on the team members. Their stories inform us of the troubles that refugees face throughout their lives. Their suffering could be greatly reduced if we could resolve the causes of inequality around the world.

Haitian, Cuban, Venezuelan, and Nicaraguan people carry their belongings as they cross the Rio Grande River. They are looking for a better life in the US.

Comprehension

A   Circle T (true) or F (false) for Sentences 1–2, complete Sentences 3–4, and answer Questions 5–6.

1. Inequality is one of the factors that creates refugees.   T / F

2. The number of refugees around the world has been decreasing.   T / F

3. 24 million refugees ...
   a. were recorded in 2010.
   b. was the highest number on record.
   c. returned to their home countries.
   d. left Pakistan in 2020.

4. Refugees have left their countries because of ...
   a. a decrease in human rights violations.
   b. unfair treatment in their home countries.
   c. better-paying jobs in other countries.
   d. the lack of education opportunities.

5. What are the two types of inequality in education that are mentioned in the passage?

6. What is the effect of the formation of the IOC Refugee Olympic Team?

B   Listen to the audio and write what you hear.   B 07-08

1.

2.

Extension

A Read the instructions and write your answers/findings. Then, discuss them with your classmates.

1. About 1% of people around the world are said to own almost 40% of the wealth around the world. What do you think about it?

2. Income inequality exists in every country. Research the situation in your country.

B Do you see or experience any inequality such as gender, income, and education in your life? Write an example and your idea about the reasons/causes behind it.

Example

Reasons/Causes

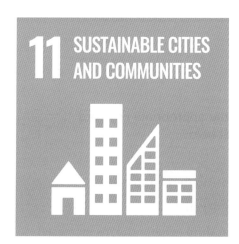

Unit 11

Sustainable Cities and Communities

Write answers for the following questions. Then, ask the questions to your partner.

1. Do you like the community you live in now? Why or why not?

2. What are typical problems of big cities?

3. What are the three most important factors for people to live happily in a community?

Vocabulary

Read the sentences with the six keywords. Then, write the appropriate keyword next to each definition or synonym ⓢ and antonym ⓐ set below.

B 09

- People in **urban** areas have very different lives from those in the countryside.
- New **migrants** to cities often lack the money needed for decent housing.
- As the economy declined, the amount of people living in **slum** neighborhoods increased.
- The construction company will **upgrade** the old roads to handle more traffic.
- What **practical** things would improve the quality of life in our cities?
- He became a **resident** of this town last year.

1. _____ [adjective] realistic and useful

2. _____ [adjective] relating to a city or built-up area

3. _____ [noun] person who lives in a certain area

4. _____ [adjective] relating to an area with low-quality, crowded conditions

5. _____ [noun] people who move from one place to another

6. _____ [verb] ⓢ improve ↔ ⓐ damage

Note-taking

Read the tip below. Then, listen to the audio and practice taking notes. Write the appropriate symbol in the [   ].

B 10

Use more symbols!
In Unit 8, you learned that using symbols can save time in note-taking.
The following list includes a few more examples.

World Urban Population

1) Ppl   rural → cities   since early _____

2) 2009   urban [   ] rural

3) Urbanization:

   • More ppl in low-_____ housing

   • [   ] air pollution, inadequate trans, lack _____

      – e.g. UN data in 2019 (> _____ cities):

         1/2 pop _____ access to public trans

Useful Symbols	
↑	increase, more, up
↓	decrease, down, less, reduce
=	are/is, equal to, have, the same as
≠	not equal to, not the same as, unequal to
>	bigger than, exceed, more than
<	less than, smaller than

Useful Abbreviations	
conv = convenient
e.g. = for example
HCS = health care service
pop = population
ppl = people
qual = quality
trans = transportation

Shadowing

 A Read the tip below. Then, practice shadowing the sentences by following Steps 1–5 on page 8.

B
11-12

Pronunciation Tip

Prepositions such as "of" and "in" are often pronounced quickly and weakly.

Ex "I've got *to* go."
"That's *for* sure."

1. People have been moving *from* rural areas *to* cities.

2. Only half *of* the urban population had convenient access *to* public transportation.

People have been moving from rural areas to cities at a rapid rate since the early 1900s. In 2009, for the first time, the world **urban** population exceeded the number of people living in rural areas. Urbanization has resulted in more people living in low-quality housing. It has also increased air pollution, inadequate transportation, and a lack of health care services. For example, UN data in 2019 from more than 600 cities found that only half of the urban population had convenient access to public transportation. Some new **migrants** have no choice but these low-cost, overcrowded areas. A recent statistic shows that more than 1 billion people around the world lived in urban **slum** housing in 2018. Rather than **upgrade** slum areas, some governments routinely destroy them. This results in many people losing their housing.

On the other hand, SDG 11 is being achieved in some places. The "City Without Slums" project was started in Surabaya by the Indonesian government in 2017. **Practical** basic services were provided, including paved paths, water drainage, public toilets, and elementary schools. The project is managed by the community, and jobs are created for **residents**. The local sense of pride in the project has an even greater positive effect on the economy of Surabaya. It is hoped that the project can be a model for future sustainable cities.

Poor local housing conditions in a slum neighborhood contrast with the more expensive high-rise developments in the background in Manila, Philippines.

Comprehension

A Circle T (true) or F (false) for Sentences 1–2 and answer Questions 3–6.

1. More people lived in the countryside than in cities in 2009.   T / F

2. In 2018, more than 1 billion people worldwide lived in low-cost, overcrowded   T / F
   urban areas.

3. Which of the following is NOT mentioned as an effect of rapid urbanization?
   a. Increased amount of slum housing
   b. Poor air quality
   c. Few employment opportunities
   d. Insufficient roads and transportation

4. What is the Indonesian government doing in Surabaya?
   a. Encouraging residents to move back to rural areas
   b. Moving the residents to another part of the city
   c. Destroying and rebuilding the area
   d. Improving the existing community

5. What problems are caused by destroying slum housing areas?

6. What are two effects of the City Without Slums project?

B Listen to the audio and write what you hear.

B
14-15

1.

2.

Extension

A Read the instructions and write your answers/findings. Then, discuss them with your classmates.

1. There are many projects for achieving SDG 11 around the world. Search with the words [sustainable cities] and choose one project. What is the project name? What is it about?

2. The decrease of the population in rural areas is problematic in many countries. What are the causes?

B Think of a village or town in your country where some improvements are necessary. Write an example and your idea to solve the problem.

Example

Solution

Responsible Consumption and Production

Warm-up

Write answers for the following questions. Then, ask the questions to your partner.

1. Where do you buy your clothes most often? Why?

2. When you buy clothes, do you check where they are made? In which countries are many of your clothes produced?

3. What does it mean to be a "responsible consumer"?

Vocabulary

Read the sentences with the six keywords. Then, write the appropriate keyword next to each definition or synonym ⓢ and antonym ⓐ set below.

B 16

- When we build roads, we often **neglect** the habitat of animals.
- The increased daily **consumption** of water has become a problem.
- The cost of household electrical **appliances** seems to go up every year.
- Garbage that is not recycled ends up as **landfill** in many cases.
- **Primarily**, the goal of the organization is to reduce the amount of e-waste.
- Charging money for plastic bags is meant to raise **awareness** of the pollution problem.

1. [noun] area of land made from waste

2. [noun] knowledge of a situation or fact

3. [noun] types of equipment designed for specific tasks

4. [noun] action of using up resources or products

5. [adverb] for the most part

6. [verb] ⓢ ignore ↔ ⓐ look after

Note-taking

Read the tip below. Then, listen to the audio and practice taking notes.

B 17

Leave a space!
If there are some words you can't hear, you can leave a space and put a question mark. Then, later you can look up what you didn't catch.

Economic Growth

Useful Abbreviations

apl = appliance
comp = computer
cons = consumption
env = environment
HH = household
negl = neglect
prob = problem
prod = product
         produce
         production
rcl = recycle
SP = smartphone
val = valuable

- Climate & pollution: _____ for economy

- Cause env prob = Irresponsible _____ & _____ of goods

- e.g. E-waste: SP, _____, _____ apl

  – ____ kg   prod/person   2019

  – Val metals   rcl & reused

  – Only ____ kg/person   rcl in env-responsible way

Shadowing

A Read the tip below. Then, practice shadowing the sentences by following Steps 1–5 on page 8.

B
18-19

Pronunciation Tip

When a voiced fricative sound such as [v], [z], or [ð] is followed by a voiceless consonant such as [k], [t], or [s], the voiced sound often becomes voiceless.

Ex [v] → [f] sound in "o*f* course"
[z] → [s] sound in "ha*s* to"

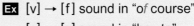

1. The main causes are the irresponsible consumption and production o*f* goods.

2. What happen*s* to our old smartphones?

B Practice shadowing the passage by following Steps 1–5 on page 8.

B
20

Many people believe that economic growth is the most important factor in human well-being. However, climate and pollution issues tend to be **neglected** for our economy to do well. The main causes of these environmental problems are the irresponsible **consumption** and production of goods. One important example is e-waste. What happens to our old smartphones, computers, and household **appliances** when we are finished with them? 7.3 kg of e-waste was produced per person in 2019. We may think that valuable metals, such as gold and copper, are recycled and reused in new products. In fact, only 1.7 kg of e-waste per person was recycled in an environmentally-responsible way. Sadly, most of us don't know that the amount of e-waste per person is growing faster than it can be recycled. A huge amount of our e-waste ends up as **landfill**. This results in chemicals and metals polluting the soil and groundwater.

The Tokyo 2020 Medal Project **primarily** aimed to raise **awareness** of the issue of e-waste. Almost 80,000 tons of small electronic devices were collected and recycled. Enough precious material was obtained to create the 5,000 gold, silver, and bronze medals needed for the winners. The project was unique as the medals were made from recycled materials for the first time in the history of the Olympics. Such awareness campaigns hope to change our attitudes about consumption.

A giant sculpture of the G7 leaders made of discarded electronic materials in St. Ives, UK. It highlights the growing threat of e-waste on the planet.

Comprehension

  Circle T (true) or F (false) for Sentences 1–2 and answer Questions 3–6.

1. In many cases, the economy is taken more seriously than environmental issues. T / F

2. The way we make and use products has a negative effect on the environment. T / F

3. Which of the following sentences is true about e-waste?
   a. The amount of e-waste that each person creates is increasing.
   b. Most e-waste is recycled.
   c. All e-waste ends up as landfill.
   d. We recycle only gold, silver, and bronze found in e-waste.

4. What was the main purpose of the Tokyo 2020 Medal Project?
   a. To demonstrate the best way to recycle old phones
   b. To save money by using recycled metal for the medals
   c. To show that e-waste is a critical problem
   d. To ensure that the athletes were recycling their garbage

5. What is the problem with e-waste left as landfill?

6. How was the Tokyo 2020 Medal Project unique?

B Listen to the audio and write what you hear. B 21-22

1.

2.

Extension

A Read the instructions and write your answers/findings. Then, discuss them with your classmates.

1. People often talk about the fast fashion industry being problematic. Research some problems about it.

2. Research some fast fashion companies that incorporate SDGs and choose one of them. What is the company name? What are they trying to do?

B Look for an example of "FAIRTRADE" products. Then, write your opinion on how you can contribute to this business model as a consumer.

Example

Contribution

Climate Action

Write answers for the following questions. Then, ask the questions to your partner.

1. Have you experienced any extreme weather? What happened? Describe the situation.

2. What are the effects of climate change? Give some examples observed around the world.

3. What has caused climate change? Choose the correct answer.

The cause of climate change is (human activities / the earth's natural system).

Vocabulary

Read the sentences with the six keywords. Then, write the appropriate keyword next to each definition or synonym ⓢ and antonym ⓐ set below.

B 23

- **Extreme** weather in the area may damage a lot of houses.
- The **drought** continued for two months until it finally rained.
- Helicopters are now needed to **combat** wildfires made worse by global warming.
- If we reduce the use of fossil fuels, what would the **impact** be on the air?
- **Commitment** from the government is necessary to switch to clean energy sources.
- A cold spring and summer resulted in a **steep** rise in the cost of vegetables.

....

1. _____ [verb]   try to reduce or eliminate something bad

2. _____ [noun]   activity or dedication to achieve a goal

3. _____ [noun]   long period of time or condition with very little or no rain

4. _____ [noun]   ⓢ effect   ↔   ⓐ cause

5. _____ [adjective] ⓢ rapid   ↔   ⓐ gradual

6. _____ [adjective] ⓢ excessive   ↔   ⓐ moderate

• •

Note-taking

Read the tip below. Then, listen to the audio and practice taking notes.
Write the appropriate symbol in the [   ].

B 24

Use your notebook efficiently!
It is important to organize information while writing it down. If you listen to a number first, you can write it on the left side, and use the right side for other information.

Combat Climate Crisis

Useful Abbreviations
agrmt = agreement
bil = billion
CC = climate change
cntry = country
emis = emission
neg = negative
US = the United States

1) _____ cntry   Paris Agrmt   2015

   • ↓ _____ impacts CC

   • Make commitments [   ] emis

2) e.g. Emis from fossil fuels in US

   • ____ bil metric tons   2005

   • ↓ by 26%   by _____

   • ↓ 5.2 & ____ bil metric tons   2012 & _____

Shadowing

 Read the tip below. Then, practice shadowing the sentences by following Steps 1–5 on page 8.

Pronunciation Tip

A phrase consisting of two words is often written as one word. You may think the pronunciation is the same, but the stress is different in many cases. Also, the meanings of two-word phrases and compound words can be different.

Ex [Two-word Phrases] "black bóard" "green hóuse"

     [Compound Words] "bláckboard" "gréenhouse"

1. The number of storms and w*i*ldfires around the planet is at an all-time high.

2. Gréenhouse gas emissions continue to drop in developed countries.

B Practice shadowing the passage by following Steps 1–5 on page 8.

B 27

The decade starting in 2011 was the warmest on record, largely because of greenhouse gas emissions.* In 2020, the average global temperature was about 14.9 degrees Celsius. This is only 1.2 degrees above the temperatures recorded at the end of the 19th century. However, this small change is responsible for the increase in **extreme** weather around the world. The number of storms, floods, **droughts**, and wildfires is at an all-time high. The largest source of greenhouse gas emissions is caused by human activities. For example, the majority of emissions come from burning fossil fuels for transportation and electricity.

To **combat** the climate crisis, 196 countries signed the Paris Agreement in 2015. The purpose is to reduce the negative **impacts** of climate change. In the agreement, countries that produce large amounts of greenhouse gases are required to make their own **commitments** to decrease their emissions. For example, emissions from burning fossil fuels in the US were 6 billion metric tons in 2005. The US promised to reduce its emissions from this level by 26% by 2025. Then, they dropped to 5.2 and 5.1 billion metric tons in 2012 and 2019, respectively. This is largely due to a **steep** drop in coal-powered electricity generation in the US. It is also due to a stronger interest in renewable energy sources. Although greenhouse gas emissions continue to drop in developed countries, they are still rising in developing countries.

*Greenhouse gas emissions include carbon dioxide that is released into the atmosphere. These emissions are the main cause of global warming.

A polar bear and her cubs travel over the ice in Nunavut, Canada. They are quickly losing their icy habitat in the Arctic Circle due to the effects of global warming.

Comprehension

A   Circle T (true) or F (false) for Sentences 1–2 and answer Questions 3–6.

1. Greenhouse gas emissions are the main cause of increased temperatures worldwide.   T / F

2. An average rise in temperature of 1.2 degrees Celsius has had little effect.   T / F

3. Which of the following is NOT an effect of climate change?
   a. A lack of rain for a long period of time
   b. Too much rainfall in one specific area
   c. The burning of fossil fuels for heat
   d. An increase in the number of fires

4. What has been an effect of the Paris Agreement?
   a. All countries have eliminated greenhouse gas emissions.
   b. The amount of greenhouse gas emissions have remained the same.
   c. The US has reduced its greenhouse gas emissions.
   d. Developing countries have reduced their greenhouse gas emissions.

5. What human activities increase greenhouse gas emissions?

6. What are two reasons that emissions have been decreasing in the US since 2012?

B   Listen to the audio and write what you hear.

B
28-29

1.

2.

Extension

A Read the instructions and write your answers/findings. Then, discuss them with your classmates.

1. Humans produce more greenhouse gases than the earth can regenerate. Research the "Earth Overshoot Day" and find out what it means. What "date" is set for this year?

2. What are solutions to climate change? Research some information about it.

B The primary source of greenhouse gas emissions is CO_2 and we have to reduce its emissions as soon as possible. What can you do in your daily life? Think of your own project and write the details such as who will be involved and what you will do.

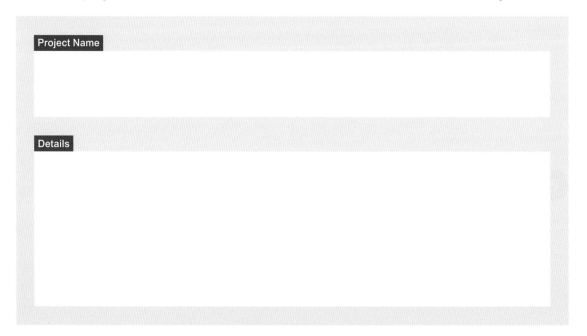

Project Name

Details

Unit 14

Life below Water

....

Warm-up

Write answers for the following questions. Then, ask the questions to your partner.

1. Do you like seafood? If yes, what kinds of seafood do you like to eat? If no, why not?

2. What problems do you think today's oceans face?

3. What human activities can affect the oceans and marine life?

Vocabulary

Read the sentences with the six keywords. Then, write the appropriate keyword next to each definition or synonym ⓢ and antonym ⓐ set below.

B 30

- There is a wide variety of **marine** plants and animals in coral reef areas.
- Some human activities **threaten** the health of the environment.
- Please don't **discard** any garbage in the river.
- The city government plans to **ban** single-use plastic products by 2025.
- It would be best to **regulate** the number of fishing boats in the area.
- We need to **enforce** the law against polluting oceans.

1. _____ [verb]   make rules about something

2. _____ [verb]   throw out something that is not useful

3. _____ [verb]   cause something to be at risk

4. _____ [adjective]   relating to or found in the sea

5. _____ [verb]   ensure that rules are followed

6. _____ [verb]   ⓢ prohibit ↔ ⓐ allow

Note-taking

Read the tip below. Then, listen to the audio and practice taking notes.

B 31

Use T-charts!
Creating a T-chart helps you to understand the similarities and differences between/among items. You can organize information in a table while listening to a passage or after listening to it.

Reduce Marine Plastic Waste

Country	Solution	Year
CN	• ban _____ plst waste	2018
_____	• ban widespread use plst bags	_____
_____	• _____ m/c into busy riv	_____
	• remove _____ kg plst every day	

Useful Abbreviations

CL = Chile
CN = China
ID = Indonesia
imp = import
m/c = machine
plst = plastic
riv = river
SP = solar power

Shadowing

A Read the tip below. Then, practice shadowing the sentences by following Steps 1–5 on page 8.

Pronunciation Tip

A letter "t" or a series of "tt" between vowels is often pronounced like [d] or [r]. This sound change is called "flap t."

Ex [t] sound in "ci*t*y"
[t] sound in "le*tt*er"

1. It is designed to remove 50,000 kg of plastic from the wa*t*er every day.

2. Governments are starting to be*tt*er enforce these laws.

B Practice shadowing the passage by following Steps 1–5 on page 8.

More than 3 billion people worldwide depend on the oceans for survival. However, **marine** life is being **threatened** by human activities. First, humans **discard** at least 8 million metric tons of used plastic products into the oceans every year. Much of this comes from factories and garbage disposal plants. Almost 80% of the plastic products in the oceans comes from rivers. The products break down into tiny microplastics that enter the food chain*. These cause serious health problems for all living things. Overfishing is also one of the biggest problems. Humans have caught too much marine life. As a result, some types of fish are in danger of extinction.

To reduce marine plastic waste, China has **banned** the import of most plastic waste products from other countries since 2018. Chile became the first South American country to ban the widespread use of plastic bags in 2018. In Indonesia, a solar-powered machine was introduced into a busy river in Jakarta in 2019. It is designed to remove 50,000 kg of plastic from the water every day. As for the overfishing problem, current international laws **regulate** the amount of fishing per season. Now governments around the world are starting to better **enforce** these laws. In addition, almost 18,000 Marine Protected Areas have been established. In those areas, human activity like fishing is limited to allow all living things to exist in harmony.

....

*The food chain describes the system of how living things depend on other living things for food. For example, plants are eaten by small fish that are eaten by bigger fish, and these are eaten by humans.

An endangered Hawksbill Sea Turtle is cut free from a discarded fishing net in Krabi, Thailand. Human actions have had a devastating effect on marine life around the world.

Comprehension

A Circle T (true) or F (false) for Sentences 1–2, complete Sentence 3, and answer Questions 4–6.

1. More than 8 million metric tons of plastic end up in the oceans every year. T / F

2. Humans end up eating microplastics in seafood. T / F

3. The main idea of the passage is that humans …
   - **a.** are becoming sick by eating fish from the oceans.
   - **b.** are eating less seafood because it includes microplastics.
   - **c.** have stopped throwing plastic garbage into rivers and oceans.
   - **d.** have damaged marine life but also proposed some solutions.

4. Which of the following is mentioned about overfishing?
   - **a.** Laws controlling which countries are allowed to fish
   - **b.** Rules enforcing the amount of marine life that can be caught
   - **c.** Types of fish that are becoming extinct
   - **d.** Marine Protected Areas prohibiting all fishing activities

5. How did Jakarta clean up one of its rivers?

6. Why are Marine Protected Areas important?

B Listen to the audio and write what you hear.

B
35-36

1.

2.

Extension

A Read the instructions and write your answers/findings. Then, discuss them with your classmates.

1. Research the "Marine Stewardship Council" and find out what they do.

2. The number of large fish has been decreasing. Search for the reasons and negative effects on biodiversity in the oceans.

B What can we do to save the oceans? Think of your own project and write the details.

Project Name

Details

Unit **15**

Life on Land

Write answers for the following questions. Then, ask the questions to your partner.

1. Do you know which animals are endangered?

2. What are the causes of these animals becoming endangered?

3. Many species are disappearing from the earth. How does it affect your life?

Vocabulary

Read the sentences with the six keywords. Then, write the appropriate keyword next to each definition or synonym Ⓢ and antonym Ⓐ set below.

B 37

- The panda's **habitat** is most often a dense bamboo forest.
- Due to climate change, the rare plant is now in danger of **extinction**.
- Most of the farmland in this region is **concentrated** near the river.
- Governments must **collaborate** with local communities on land improvement projects.
- Activists gathered to **halt** the highway construction to save the wildlife in the area.
- The organization's goal is to **restore** the animal population in the grassland.

1. _____ [verb]   work together for a purpose

2. _____ [adjective] relating to a high proportion of something in one area

3. _____ [noun]   situation where a species no longer exists

4. _____ [noun]   natural home of a living thing

5. _____ [verb]   return something back to its original condition

6. _____ [verb]   Ⓢ stop ↔ Ⓐ continue

Note-taking

Review the Note-taking tips you have learned. Then, listen to the audio and take notes. Share your notes with your classmates.

B 38

Transportation Project in Africa

Shadowing

 A Read the tip below. Then, practice shadowing the sentences by following Steps 1–5 on page 8.

B
39-40

Pronunciation Tip

When [t], [d], and [s] are followed by [j], two sounds are often assimilated.

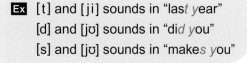

Ex [t] and [ji] sounds in "last year"
[d] and [jʊ] sounds in "did you"
[s] and [jʊ] sounds in "makes you"

1. The people there are not yet able to manage the land well.
2. The benefits of restoring the land are not yet fully realized.

B Practice shadowing the passage by following Steps 1–5 on page 8.

Globally, almost 100 million hectares of forest were lost in the two decades since 2000: The size is about 2.5 times the area of Japan. Deforestation* lowers the quality of the soil. It also has negative effects on biodiversity* and animal **habitats**. As a result, the risk of plant and animal **extinction** has increased by about 10% since 1990. The area of forest land actually increased slightly since 2000 in Asia, Europe, and North America. However, significant losses were **concentrated** in South America and Sub-Saharan Africa. Climate change and deforestation have resulted in about a 10% increase in the size of the Sahara Desert since 1920. The population growth in this area is also one reason for the desertification. Moreover, the people there are not yet able to manage the land well.

Since 2007, 20 African countries have **collaborated** with the African Union to **halt** the spread of the desert. They planned a Great Green Wall 8,000 km across the whole continent of Africa, just south of the Sahara Desert. The goal of the project is to **restore** 100 million hectares of desert land with trees and plants by 2030. Close to 18% had already been completed in 2020. The project has also created over 350,000 jobs in local communities. While the benefits of restoring the land are not yet fully realized, the first important steps have been made.

*Deforestation is the widespread clearing of forest areas, due to agriculture and urbanization in most cases.
*Biodiversity means the variety of life existing together in one ecosystem.

Trees are planted in Qinghai, China to control the spread of the desert. Tree planting is part of the country's plan to reduce greenhouse gas emissions.

Comprehension

 A Circle T (true) or F (false) for Sentences 1–2, complete Sentences 3–4, and answer Questions 5–6.

1. Decreasing biodiversity could result in some types of animals or plants dying out. T / F

2. The amount of forest land in Asia has increased since the year 2000. T / F

3. Deforestation does NOT affect ...
   a. the varieties of plants and animals.
   b. the natural homes of many animals.
   c. the overall health of the forest ground.
   d. the population growth of humans.

4. The Great Green Wall will ...
   a. replace the Sahara Desert in Africa.
   b. create jobs for people living in Africa.
   c. extend to deserts in other continents.
   d. have a negative effect on biodiversity.

5. What are four factors causing desertification?

6. What is being done to restore the land just south of the Sahara Desert?

B Listen to the audio and write what you hear.

B
42-43

1.

2.

Extension

A Read the instructions and write your answers/findings. Then, discuss them with your classmates.

1. What are the causes of deforestation around the world?

2. What does "FSC" stand for? What is its main purpose?

B Do you see any evidence of deforestation around you? Write an example and your idea to solve the problem.

Example

Solution

Unit 16

Peace, Justice and Strong Institutions

Write answers for the following questions. Then, ask the questions to your partner.

1. Imagine your country is at war. What kind of life would you have?

2. There are many armed conflicts going on around the world. Do you know any examples?

3. The word "justice" in SDG 16 means the act of being fair and ethical. Is it important for you? Why or why not?

Vocabulary

Read the sentences with the six keywords. Then, write the appropriate keyword next to each definition or synonym ⓢ and antonym ⓐ set below.

B
44

- Our presentation on human rights is **inclusive** of everyone's ideas and opinions.
- Soldiers are **defenders** of the people in their countries.
- The **journalist** reported the events accurately in her articles.
- A national **institution** was set up to monitor students' abilities with language.
- The **independent** news website is not influenced by the government.
- The organization is investigating some **complaints** about police violence.

1. _____ [noun]   person who writes for newspapers or news websites

2. _____ [noun]   statements showing that something is unacceptable

3. _____ [adjective] involving all or almost all

4. _____ [noun]   organization for a social purpose

5. _____ [adjective] ⓢ free   ↔   ⓐ controlled

6. _____ [noun]   ⓢ protectors ↔ ⓐ attackers

Note-taking

Review the Note-taking tips you have learned. Then, listen to the audio and take notes. Share your notes with your classmates.

B
45

National Human Rights Institutions

Shadowing

 A Read the tip below. Then, practice shadowing the sentences by following Steps 1–5 on page 8.

B
46-48

> **Pronunciation Tip**
>
> When an [n] sound is followed by a [p], [b], or [m] sound, [n] often changes to [m] because of assimilation.
>
> **Ex** [n] → [m] sound in "i*n* person"
> [n] → [m] sound in "i*n* brief"
> [n] → [m] sound in "o*n* my own"

1. I*n* particular, these include the freedom of religion, thought, expression, and privacy.
2. Many more have bee*n* put into prison for their political views.
3. I*n* many cases, they are not allowed access to lawyers or their embassies.

B Practice shadowing the passage by following Steps 1–5 on page 8.

Everyone deserves human rights. In particular, these include the freedom of religion, thought, expression, and privacy. Respecting human rights would go a long way in creating more peaceful, fair, and **inclusive** societies. Unfortunately, there are many human rights abuses around the world. Since 2015, almost 2,000 human rights **defenders** and **journalists** have been killed in domestic or international conflicts. Many more have been put into prison for their political views or actions against human rights abuses. In many cases, they are not allowed access to lawyers or their embassies. There are likely more cases than reported, as victims are often too afraid to report the abuses.

The UN stresses that National Human Rights **Institutions** are essential in defending human rights in all countries. They should be **independent** from governments, so their actions can't be controlled. One example is the National Human Rights Commission in India, established in 1993. It deals with a wide range of human rights **complaints**. The institution received more than 75,000 complaints in 2020. Their investigations cover cases of labor management, refugee rights, child labor, and violence by the police. They also support rights for disabled people and the elderly. As of 2021, only 118 countries around the word have official institutions, but the number is slowly increasing now.

Youth in London, UK take part in a Black Lives Matter protest. The worldwide protests raised awareness of the discrimination faced by minority populations.

Comprehension

A Circle T (true) or F (false) for Sentences 1–2, complete Sentence 3, and answer
Questions 4–6.

1. Freedom of expression is an example of a human right.   T / F

2. Journalists don't suffer from human rights abuses.   T / F

3. The National Human Rights Commission in India ...
   - **a.** deals with cases of human rights abuses in India.
   - **b.** is an international human rights organization.
   - **c.** defends companies who break the law.
   - **d.** focuses mainly on the rights of refugees.

4. Which of the following is NOT mentioned about people who protect human rights?
   - **a.** They can be killed for their political activities.
   - **b.** They are sometimes imprisoned for their beliefs.
   - **c.** They work for government organizations.
   - **d.** They are often denied legal assistance.

5. Why are there likely more human rights abuses than reported?

6. Why should National Human Rights Institutions be independent from governments?

B Listen to the audio and write what you hear.

B
50-51

1.

2.

Extension

A Read the instructions and write your answers/findings. Then, discuss them with your classmates.

1. What do you think about "human trafficking"? How and why is it happening?

2. Research some information about "child soldiers." Then, find out where and why many children have to become soldiers.

B Suppose you will teach about wars at an elementary school in order to raise awareness of the importance of peace. Decide on a topic and lesson type, then write details about your teaching plan.

Topic

Hiroshima / Kamikaze / soldiers' lives / war orphans / war survivors /
your own idea:

Lesson Type

discussion / guest speaker / lecture / video /
your own idea:

Teaching Plan

Partnerships for the Goals

Warm-up

Write answers for the following questions. Then, ask the questions to your partner.

1. What do you think "partnerships" mean?

2. SDG 17 is about creating partnerships to achieve SDGs 1–16. Who or what institutions could be involved in such partnerships?

3. What are the benefits of partnerships?

Vocabulary

Read the sentences with the six keywords. Then, write the appropriate keyword next to each definition or synonym ⓢ and antonym ⓐ set below.

B
52

- Trading relationships between countries are **essential** for the benefit of everyone.
- All members in the IT **cooperative** share the profits equally.
- The institute must **ensure** that each student in the district has enough stationery.
- The volunteer group is going to **export** local artwork to make money for the village.
- Some NGOs set up a fund to provide **equitable** treatment for animals in wildlife parks around the world.
- The organizations **distribute** meals to people in need.

1. _____ [verb]   give or deliver something

2. _____ [verb]   make certain that something will happen

3. _____ [noun]   group operated by co-owners or members

4. _____ [verb]   move products out of a country for trade

5. _____ [adjective] ⓢ necessary ↔ ⓐ unimportant

6. _____ [adjective] ⓢ fair ↔ ⓐ unjust

Note-taking

Review the Note-taking tips you have learned. Then, listen to the audio and take notes. Share your notes with your classmates.

B
53

Partnerships between Developing and Developed Countries

Shadowing

 A Read the tip below. Then, practice shadowing the sentences by following Steps 1–5 on page 8.   B 54-55

> **Pronunciation Tip**
>
> There are many words like "record" where the accent is put on the first syllable for nouns, and on the second syllable for verbs. When you find a word that has the same spelling for the noun/adjective and verb, make sure to check the accent.
>
> **Ex** "decrease" décrease [noun] → decréase [verb]
> "perfect" pérfect [adjective] → perféct [verb]

1. Farmers can expórt their products to developed countries for equitable prices.
2. The óbject is to reduce the technological inequalities between developing and developed countries.

B Practice shadowing the passage by following Steps 1–5 on page 8.

B
56

Partnerships are **essential** in promoting sustainable development across borders, particularly between developing and developed countries. Various types of partnerships have been created to support developing countries, including trading partnerships among others. For example, since 1997, an organization called Fairtrade International has helped to create partnerships between farm **cooperatives** in developing countries and buyers in developed countries. In 2019, more than 1.7 million farmers and workers in more than 72 countries participated in partnerships through Fairtrade. The partnerships **ensure** that farmers and workers can **export** their products to buyers in developed countries for **equitable** prices. For example, Ugandan, Ethiopian, and Tanzanian farmers are able to sell flowers to European markets. Haitian mango farmers are now exporting to the US. Myanmar cooperatives are selling coffee to French buyers.

A wide range of technical assistance and training partnerships have also been made. The object is to reduce the technological inequalities between developing and developed countries. An example of this type of partnership is a UK organization called Computer Aid. They collect and upgrade donated computers and **distribute** them to schools in over 100 countries. The organization's greatest strength is their local teacher training program. Computer Aid has helped over 14.5 million people to learn how to use computers since 1997. Partnerships through Fairtrade and Computer Aid allow people in developing countries to strengthen their communities and economies.

The owner of an Australian coffee business buys certified organic and Fairtrade coffee from farmers living high in the Andes mountains in Peru.

Comprehension

 A Circle T (true) or F (false) for Sentences 1–2 and answer Questions 3–6.

1. There are many kinds of partnerships which support developing countries.   T / F

2. Computer Aid is an American organization.   T / F

3. Which of the following sentences is true about Fairtrade's relationship with the developing countries?
   a. Fairtrade owns farm cooperatives in developing countries.
   b. Fairtrade allows farmers to get fair prices for their goods.
   c. Farmers began forming partnerships with Fairtrade in 2019.
   d. Developing countries can access financial loans from Fairtrade.

4. What is the main goal of Computer Aid?
   a. To sell computer products to people in developing countries
   b. To train teachers in developing countries to work in the UK
   c. To give more access to technology to people in developing countries
   d. To use technology to export goods to developing countries

5. What are three products mentioned as exports from developing countries?

6. What are two of Computer Aid's main activities?

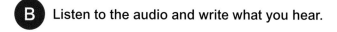 **B** Listen to the audio and write what you hear.
B
57-58

1.

2.

Extension

A Read the instructions and write your answers/findings. Then, discuss them with your classmates.

1. The SDGs are divided into 17 parts, but they are actually related to each other. Which SDGs are most closely linked? Why do you think so?

2. Partnerships are necessary to achieve the SDGs. Research a partnership between countries or in your country. What are they trying to do?

B Suppose you are a member of a volunteer group to support children from low-income families. What partnership would you create? Write your plan to support the children.

Partnership

Plan

Presentation Project

Let's make a poster presentation on one of the SDGs!

Part I

Preparation

You will learn some important elements for preparing a poster presentation in this part.

Groundwork

Making an outline is necessary before you write a script for your presentation. Here are example steps for you to follow:

Step 1 Learn about the issues first and decide on a topic. For example, you could choose "Plastic Waste."

Step 2 Brainstorm some ideas about it. Then, share your ideas with your partner. Add some more points to your list if you want.

Step 3 Categorize the ideas from the list in Step 2.

Background	Problems	Solutions	Others

Step 4 Choose one of the problems from the table above and make an outline of your presentation. You can also add other ideas to make the introduction, solution, and conclusion parts if necessary.

Introduction ▶ _____

_____

_____

Problem ▶ _____

_____

_____

Solution ▶ _____

_____

_____

Conclusion ▶ _____

_____

_____

Numbers

Using numbers and dates are very important to add credibility to your presentation.

1 Spell out the following numbers and words to make sure that you can pronounce them.

Numbers

100 ▶ *one hundred*   1,000 ▶

10,000 ▶   1,000,000 ▶

13 ▶   30 ▶   14 ▶   40 ▶

398 ▶

2,682 ▶

67,172 ▶

159,435,000 ▶

1/2 ▶   2/3 ▶   1/4 ▶

Units

2.7 kg ▶

39.56% ▶

−8°C ▶

24°F ▶

Years

1985 ▶   2001 ▶

2030 ▶   1900s ▶

2 Listen to the audio and check the pronunciation.

B
59

3 Practice saying the numbers and words above with your partner.

Graphs

Line graphs are important visual materials for your presentation and description sentences can help to explain them.

1 Fill in the blanks using the words in the box.

■ The Number of People in Extreme Poverty around the World

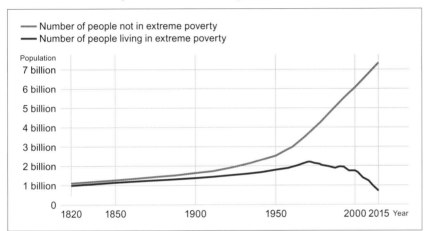

dropped
dramatically
gradually
reached
shows
x-axis
y-axis

- This graph _____ the number of people around the world who were living in extreme poverty from 1820 until 2015.
- The _____ indicates years.
- The _____ indicates the population.
- The number of people not in extreme poverty increased _____ between 1850 and 1950. After that, it increased _____. The total number _____ its peak in 2015.
- The number of people living in extreme poverty has _____ since 1975.

2 Listen to the audio and check your answers.

B
60

3 Practice saying the description sentences above with your partner.

Charts

Pie charts are important visual materials for your presentation and description sentences can help to explain them.

1 Fill in the blanks using the words in the box.

■ Women in Poverty in the US

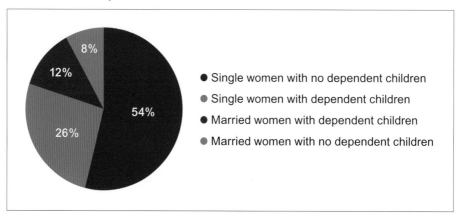

- Single women with no dependent children
- Single women with dependent children
- Married women with dependent children
- Married women with no dependent children

account	describes	of	quarter

- This pie chart _____ the percentage of women in poverty.
- 54% _____ US women in poverty are single with no dependent children.
- More than a _____ of US women in poverty are single with dependent children.
- Married women _____ for 20% of the women in poverty in the US.

2 Listen to the audio and check your answers.

B
61

3 Practice saying the description sentences above with your partner.

Tables

Tables are important visual materials for your presentation and description sentences can help to explain them.

1 Fill in the blanks using the words in the box.

■ Estimates of Poverty in India

Year	Poverty Ratio (%)			Number of Poor (in millions)		
	Rural	Urban	Combined	Rural	Urban	Combined
1973–74	56.4	49.0	54.9	261	60	321
1993–94	37.3	32.4	36.0	244	76	320
1999–00	27.1	23.6	26.1	193	67	260

column	compares	decreased	row	than

- This table _____ poverty levels in rural and urban areas in India.
- The left _____ shows the range of years.
- The first _____ shows poverty in India from 1973 to 1974.
- The poverty ratio in India _____ between 1973 and 2000.
- There is more poverty in the rural areas _____ in the urban areas.

2 Listen to the audio and check your answers.

B
62

3 Practice saying the description sentences above with your partner.

Expressions

Using typical phrases is very useful in marking transitions throughout your presentation.

1 Categorize the following typical phrases into the seven steps of a presentation.

- Greetings
- Introduction (Giving the Topic)
- Transition to the Next Idea
- Giving Details
- Referring to Information Sources
- Conclusion
- Concluding Remarks

a. According to the Oxford dictionary, …
b. First / Second / Third, …
c. Furthermore / In addition / Moreover, …
d. Hello, everyone. Let me introduce …
e. In short / In conclusion / To sum up, …
f. Let me give you some examples.
g. Now, let me go on to the next point.
h. Thank you for your attention.
i. To begin with, …
j. Today, I would like to talk about …

2 Check your answers with your partner.

3 Practice saying the typical phrases above with your partner.

Impression

Delivery, story, and visuals are three important elements that can help to make an impressive presentation.

1 Complete the chart using the words in the box.

> content
> eye contact
> gestures
> good organization
> images
> intonation
> posture
> PowerPoint
> uniqueness
> voice

Delivery	Story	Visuals

2 Check your answers with your classmates.

3 Try to add a few more ideas with your classmates. Then, discuss why each of the above elements is important.

Delivery

Using delivery skills effectively is very important to attract the attention of an audience for your presentation.

1 Suppose the following paragraph is the beginning of your presentation. Listen to the audio. Then, read it aloud and practice it using the delivery skills described below. Try to memorize the whole paragraph.

B
63

Hello, everyone. My name is (*full name*). Today, I would like to tell you about the poverty issues in our community. First, I will describe how the poverty rate is increasing here, and the reasons why this is happening. Finally, I will explain several activities that people in the community have been engaged in. Now, let me start. Here is a line graph on the screen.

2 Take turns presenting in groups. Complete the self-check after you finish your own presentation.

Delivery Skills	Self-check	Yes	Not Enough	No
Eye Contact	Did I look at everyone in the audience?			
Posture	Did I stand straight with my hands and legs in an appropriate position?			
Gesture	Did I use any gestures?			
Facial Expression	Was my facial expression friendly and confident?			
Voice	Was my voice clear and loud enough?			
Speed	Did I speak with pauses and not too fast?			

3 What will you do to improve your delivery skills in your next presentation?

Part Ⅱ
Presentation

Your goal in this part is to make a poster presentation with your classmates. Read the information below and proceed according to the steps.

Purpose

▶ Deepen understanding of SDGs

▶ Understand the current situation around the world

▶ Learn how to work together through group activities

▶ Improve communication skills

▶ Collect and process information in English

▶ Learn effective presentation methods

Overview of Steps

1. Make a small group.

2. Choose one of the SDGs to present.

3. Look for one or two visual materials.

4. Research some background information for the visual material(s).

5. Make an outline.

6. Make a poster.

7. Write a script.

8. Rehearse your presentation.

9. Make a poster presentation.

10. Reflect on your presentation.

Groundwork

A Make a small group and choose one of the SDGs to present. Then, answer the following questions.

1 Which SDG did your group choose?

SDG

2 What is one of the problems related to the SDG your group chose?

3 Look for one or two visual materials such as graphs, charts, or tables related to the problem your group chose. Then, write a description of them.

4 List the key points from your visual materials.

5 Write some ideas for a solution to the problem.

B **Using the notes you made on the previous page, make an outline of your presentation with your group members.**

Introduction ▸

Problem ▸

Description of the Visual Material(s) ▸

Key Point 1 ▸

Key Point 2 ▸

Solution ▸

Conclusion ▸

Poster

Follow the steps below to make a poster for your presentation.

Step 1 Think of the title of your presentation with your group members.

Step 2 Prepare some materials for your poster. Make sure to include the following information:

- Title
- Group Members' Names
- Introduction
- Problem
- Key Points
- Solution
- Conclusion
- Visual Material(s)
- Graphic(s) such as Photo(s) or Illustration(s)

Step 3 Make a poster.

■ Example Organization of a Poster

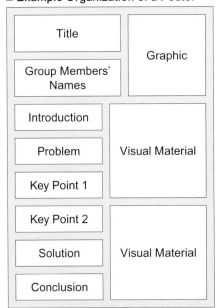

Script

A   Listen to the audio and study the organization of the script.

Hello, everyone. Thank you for your interest in our poster. Our group chose SDG 1 "No Poverty."

As you know, many people in our world are still suffering from poverty. We often see the situation in developing countries in the media, but actually poverty can be seen in developed countries as well.

Please look at this graph. The graph shows the poverty rates in Japan. This red line shows the overall poverty rate. As you can see, it has been gradually increasing. Now please look at the blue line. This shows that the child poverty rate had been increasing consistently until the year 2012, then it started to fall. In 2018, the rate was 13.5%.

One key point is that even in a developed country like Japan, there is a certain number of people living in poverty. This came as a surprise to our group because we are used to hearing about poverty in other countries. However, the Japanese poverty rate of 15% is relatively high.

Another key point is that we need to pay attention to the fact that child poverty is more than 10%. Even though it has been decreasing in the past few years, it is the responsibility of adults to help those children in need.

We should see what we can do in our local communities to help those in poverty. We all need to start thinking about how we can solve this problem. We could start volunteering with a food bank, or ask what we can do at our local community center.

In conclusion, the only way that change will come is if we take action to solve this problem. Thank you for your attention.

■ Poverty Rate in Japan

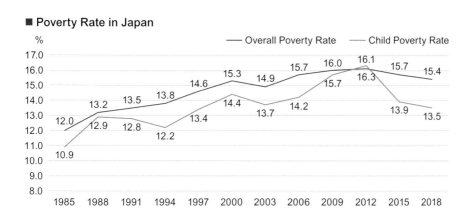

B Referring to the example on the previous page, write a script with your group members for the problem you chose.

Rehearsal

A Watch the video. Then, note four skills necessary for a successful presentation.

VIDEO

- _____
- _____
- _____
- _____

B Rehearse your script using the skills above. Speak clearly and try to keep your head up. Pay attention to your tone and pronunciation as well.

Poster Presentation

Read the following information on the day of your presentation.

Before the Presentation

1. Make sure that you have memorized the script.
2. Put your poster on a wall or desk.
3. The first presenter stays at the poster.
4. The other members visit the next location.

During the Presentation

1. When your teacher gives the class a signal, the first presenter starts presenting.
2. The first presenter repeats the presentation a few times for different visitors who rotate around the classroom.
3. When the teacher announces a presenter switch, the second presenter moves to the poster and starts presenting.
4. Continue the cycle until all group members finish presenting at least a few times.

Reflection

After the presentation, evaluate other groups using the following points.

Good Points
- appropriate visual materials
- easy to understand
- good speed
- strong voice
- comfortable attitude
- good eye contact
- interesting content
- use of gestures
- didn't use notes
- good memory
- smiling

Points to Improve
- few gestures
- no eye contact
- reading too much
- weak voice
- irrelevant visual materials
- no smiling
- too fast/slow
- needs more practice
- not well-organized
- very shy or quiet

Group Number	One Good Point	One Point to Improve	One Thing I Learned

1 How was your group's presentation?

_____

_____

2 Which group's presentation were you most interested in? Why?

_____

_____

クラス用音声CD有り（別売）

Making Choices
—Exploring Your Approach to SDGs
シャドーイングでSDGsを学び、コンピテンシーを高める

2022年2月28日　初版発行

著　者　田頭未希／Fergus Hann／藤田玲子
発行者　松村達生
発行所　センゲージ ラーニング株式会社
　　　　〒102-0073　東京都千代田区九段北1-11-11　第2フナトビル5階
　　　　電話 03-3511-4392　FAX 03-3511-4391
　　　　e-mail: elt@cengagejapan.com
　　　　copyright©2022 センゲージ ラーニング株式会社

装　丁　　足立友幸（parastyle inc.）
編集協力　飯尾緑子（parastyle inc.）
印刷・製本　株式会社エデュプレス

ISBN 978-4-86312-394-6

もし落丁、乱丁、その他不良品がありましたら、お取り替えいたします。本書の全部、または一部を無断で複写（コピー）することは、著作権法上での例外を除き、禁じられていますのでご注意ください。